Praise for *Make Your SHIFT:*

The Five Most Powerful Moves You Can Make to Get Where YOU Want to Go

"Beverly Flaxington makes a powerful contribution to the growing body of responsibility centered self-help works with *Make Your SHIFT: The Five Most Powerful Moves You Can Make to Get Where YOU Want to Go*. The most important word in 'self-help' is 'Self,' and Beverly does a wonderful job of assuring that you have control over the processes of making significant changes in your life —as long as you accept the responsibility.

"Beverly's method is direct, uncomplicated and accessible to all of us. She avoids the pseudo-psychology and mysticism that too many personal development gurus use to dazzle us. Instead she gives us a system that demands reflection while preserving engagement and offers transcendence while remaining firmly grounded.

"Change is hard work, but can be achieved by establishing attainable, realistic goals. *Make Your SHIFT: The Five Most Powerful Moves You Can Make to Get Where YOU Want to Go* nicely dispels the myth of the 'you can achieve anything' culture and offers a systematic method for identifying not only what you'd like to accomplish, but why. This book will help you identify the meaningful steps that will result in authentic change. Most of all, Beverly Flaxington gives you the tools to help you help yourself."

—*Jim Bouchard*
Speaker, Media Personality and Author of "Think Like a Black Belt"
ThinkLikeaBlackBelt.ORG

"Get ready to SHIFT! This book is action-packed and filled with excellent tools and ideas for making a needed change in your life. You can't help but take more powerful steps if you follow this clear plan for success!"

—*Tanya Paluso "Bliss"*
Co-founder and CEO of Tribal Truth

"I love this book. Beverly Flaxington has uncovered the missing piece in the countless number of goal-setting books and programs in the marketplace. Where others have failed, her holistic S.H.I.F.T.™ model offers an insightful approach to setting and accomplishing our goals with a clear sense of purpose. Encouraging us to 'look under the hood' to ask the 'why' behind the goals we set, she skillfully weaves a practical path to integrate our values, interests and motivations to the goal-setting process. Applied with discipline and drive, her strategies are sure to bring much success and newfound meaning to the lives of many. I recommend this book highly—and have many times."

— *Dan King, Principal Career Counselor and Coach,*
Career Planning and Management, Inc.

"Change is hard. Bev's process makes it much easier. The 5 steps are thoughtful, reasonable and easy to understand."

— *Teresa de Grosbois*
Word-of-mouth Marketing Expert, best-selling Author,
International Speaker and Founder of the Evolutionary Business Council

Make Your SHIFT:

The Five Most Powerful Moves You Can
Make to Get Where YOU Want to Go

Beverly D. Flaxington

ATA Press

Published by ATA Press

ISBN 978-0-9837620-2-7

Library of Congress Control Number 2011942716

First printing: January, 2012

Table of Contents

I

This book is dedicated to those people who make the shift on behalf of those with no voice of their own. I honor three inspiring women I have been blessed to know:

JOANNE WILKINSON, MD
founder of Forever Home Rescue

JUDY AMBROSE
President of the
Neponset Valley Humane Society

LYNN MARGHERIO
founder & CEO of Cradles to Crayons

Foreword

Jackie Black, Ph.D.

Author of *Meeting Your Match: Cracking the
Code to Successful Relationships* and *Couples
& Money: Cracking the Code to Ending the #1
Conflict in Marriage*

Make Your SHIFT: The Five Most Powerful Moves You Can Make to Get Where YOU Want to Go is an easy read, but don't underestimate the BIG value that Bev Flaxington weaves through every chapter of this book. This book is jam-packed with rich content, wonderful personal stories, and solid examples of every method, tool, and tip Bev created to help readers make their lives and relationships better! Her 5-Step (Shifting) Process is thoughtful and personalized so that the "Shifts" each reader wants to make can be explored by each reader taking into consideration their own resistance, obstacles, considerations, and so much more that are different for each of us! So while the themes in our lives are universal, our approach to change is personal and individual; and Bev understands that and encourages us to step into the details of our hopes and dreams and create the change that is possible for us. If you only buy one self-help or business book this year, make it this one.

Introduction

There's something very satisfying about having your house in order—literally and figuratively. Yet despite the incentive, which is that higher level of satisfaction, very few of us ever put things in place as we'd like them to be.

As an example, for some people actually being organized is an ideal goal but remains an elusive one. We might strive toward it in some way, or think "I should be more organized" or "I should be... (fill in the blank)." In too many cases, we want it, but we do not get it. With hundreds if not thousands of self-help books out there, you would think more people might actually be getting to where they want to be! It begs the question, if people actually want to achieve something different, why are so few of us actually getting there?

Deep down, it could be that many of us really do not want to be in control (almost) of our own lives or take the steps necessary to gain that control. Perhaps most of us never get focused enough because we sabotage our own efforts; and subconsciously, this focus is not what we want. We actually resist what we say we desire, in some cases.

Let's face it—if you do not actually focus on something you really want, or if you are focusing on something you only think you want, subconsciously you may stop yourself en route to where you are headed. An old friend of mine once said, "Some people like their pain and do not want to alleviate it!"

I believe that in many cases we do desire this new state, but simply have not been taught a process or approach that we can apply in our own lives to get there. We can read the books of experts telling us what to do, but I think most approaches that have come before the S.H.I.F.T. Model™ miss a key element. Very few of these books actually take the single most important factor into account: human nature.

Instead of helping you understand your own nature and how you can work with it to create positive changes in your life, most books gloss over the importance of *you* altogether. They offer a step-by-step approach, or a set of instructions, or a deep theoretical perspective, but they don't address what holds most of us back—our own nature.

Think about it for a minute. If you have read a book or magazine article on goal setting and personal development, you have probably come across the standard approach to goal setting and planning that features in just about every one of the hundreds of thousands of goal-setting and self-improvement books on the proverbial bookshelf.

Be SMART!

One standard approach to goal setting, for instance, tells you to set SMART goals. This is a summary of good goal setting that says you need your goals to be (1) specific, (2) measurable, (3) attainable, (4) realistic, and (5) time-bound. It is a great guideline to think about how to construct a goal. Instead of "I want to lose weight," a SMART goal would be "I want to lose four pounds over the next two months by working out at the gym three times a week for 45 minutes." It takes something that is general and makes it very specific.

Beyond this, though, the process of actually losing those four pounds can break down. You have written a clear goal, but sustaining the change effort is often left to chance, and this is the real problem. The steps of figuring out why you have not been able to attain this goal in the past, or what holds you back personally, don't even get addressed.

Human beings are responsible for change, whether it is change in their personal or their professional life. Every effort to create change, however, is susceptible to the same problem — lack of commitment and motivation. Change requires the motivation to keep up a sustained effort, and a commitment to getting to the desired place. And it requires a level of awareness, understanding, buy-in, and action.

Think about whatever you are looking to change about your life. Where are you in your process? The key ideas offered in this book can set you on the road to success. The proven method will help you to sustain commitment to your goals and to maintain your focus on the overall planned outcome, no matter how unsuccessful you have been in the past.

In the last twenty-five years, I have taken on many roles — in business and in working with individuals as a hypnotherapist — that have allowed me to observe many individuals intent on achieving personal change. I am, or have been, a hypnotherapist, a corporate consultant, a senior-level executive, a college professor, and a professional coach.

What Has Been Missing?

From these various vantage points, I have seen firsthand how and why the standard approaches to goal setting and goal achievement simply do not work. It is not that any classic goal setting provides false information. It is not even that people do not have some idea about the importance of taking what I call disciplined action. Rather, the many standard approaches to goal setting and achievement simply miss the key aspects of how we operate as human beings—how we can really determine what we want, how we stay motivated, and what change can mean for each of us in the long term.

With this book, then, and its business-focused companion, *Make the SHIFT: The Proven Five-Step Plan to Success for Corporate Teams*, for the first time ever, you're getting access to a seminal process tailored specifically to help you make positive changes effectively.

This book looks at everything from the resistance to success we all experience and ways to break free of it, right down to the issues relating to what you want, your desired outcomes, and how they can sometimes be in conflict.

The ideas I'm talking about here are also outlined in a step-by-step fashion so you can put them into practice right away. They are not esoteric theories or complicated concepts, but rather clear steps you can take to shift your life in a new direction in no time.

A few words of advice, though. First, as you read through the process, take the time to complete each step. Second, remember that going through the process and applying it to your own experience is the key to success in your shift. Getting from here to there, from A to B, is never easy, so realize that at the outset. But change can happen—I've seen hundreds and hundreds of people do it with this guide.

Book Structure

This book is divided into two sections. Part I discusses the specific steps of implementing the proven five-step process of making your shift, and Part II discusses helpful tips and tools that have worked for literally thousands of people I have shared them with over the years.

Part I is arranged as a step-by-step process with specific elements to focus on in sequential order. The S.H.I.F.T. Model™ 5-step process is intended to be used in order—the first step is labeled as "S," the next as "H," and so on. The process was created as a change model, so it works for anything you need to change—from something simple like getting along with a colleague, to far more complicated tasks like changing your lifestyle to be healthier, happier, and more productive. The only thing that changes is the manner in which you approach the steps. That will differ depending on your end goal. Do not skip any of the steps, though, because it will mean that you do not develop a plan as thoroughly as you should.

At the end of Part I, you will have everything in place to finally make the successful leap—a leap you may have tried unsuccessfully before—from where you are now to where you want to be.

Part II is structured in a looser format, with methods, tools, and tips that will make your transition more productive. Learning and internalizing them will make the shifting process easier and more effective.

It is possible to read either Part I or Part II of this book separately, because both parts are designed to work as stand-alone reference works, but they complement each other too, so the second strengthens the effect of the first.

In any event, whatever you do, it is important to commit to do something. I've seen situations in which someone made even a minor shift—learned to do just one thing better and more effectively in their life—and created a ripple effect that made many areas of their life better. I hope you feel inspired to do the same.

So whether you are looking to shift your life by changing jobs, learning something new, losing weight, getting a new job, or perhaps getting a better handle on your finances, there's no time like the present.

Let's get started!

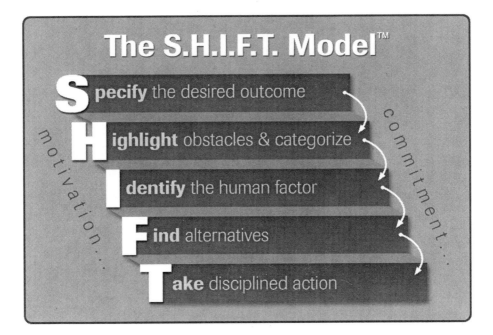

The S.H.I.F.T. Model™

Specify the desired outcome

Highlight obstacles & categorize

Identify the human factor

Find alternatives

Take disciplined action

motivation...

commitment...

PART I

The S.H.I.F.T. Model™

The S.H.I.F.T. Model™ is the result of decades of working with individuals and businesses. Over the years, I began to notice, when I worked with clients on change management, that I was taking the same steps to uncover real workable solutions as I did when working with individuals through coaching, hypnosis, training, or other behavioral change initiatives. The steps may seem almost self-evident once you understand them, but many of us simply can't afford to take the time to look up from the daily grind long enough to see the obvious.

As we said in the introduction, most efforts to bring about change do not take the actual process of change into consideration. They do not help you take the necessary steps to become and remain committed to change, seeing it through from start to finish.

Introduction to the S.H.I.F.T. Model™

T he first step in the S.H.I.F.T. Model™ is Specifying the Desired Outcome. It sounds simple enough. Unfortunately, a common mistake is to assume that it is as simple as it sounds. Being able to specify what you want and, even more to the point, identifying something that you actually want to achieve, requires a very focused effort. To be able to specify desired outcomes, you need to "know thyself," as the Delphic Oracle commanded. To know yourself, however, and your own mind, you have to take the time to really think through what you want in your life.

My approach to this first step in the change process picks up on this principle. It always starts with defining exactly what you want to achieve in your life—and very importantly, why you want to achieve it. Often I find a lack of response or clarity about what success really means. Defining the goal carefully and with exactitude is the first crucial step in any change effort.

The second step in the process is to Highlight and Categorize the

Obstacles to Change. This process of clearly and deliberately identifying obstacles is important to uncover what is or may be standing between where you are and where you want to be. Depending on your goals and where you're starting from, these obstacles could include things like family, relationships, money, work, and even more internal issues, such as your own confidence and ability to believe in yourself.

I often see my clients assuming that they will just forge ahead and tackle whatever gets in their way, but they try to move forward without any conception that there are inevitably things that are going to slow their progress, potentially forcing them to rethink their precise direction. Obstacles are inevitable if you do not think ahead, and they are often the same obstacles you have encountered repeatedly. This is one of the main reasons people do not achieve their goals. When they find the same obstacles rearing up again and again, their commitment to change starts to diminish.

Defining the obstacles beforehand, however, lets you capture and categorize what you must plan for ahead of time. It also lets you identify those things that are out of your control, so you do not waste your resources and time worrying about them. Recognizing them in advance allows you to plan a different means of achieving your goals. You might try to find a way to work around your obstacle with focus. Or, staying on the same path, you might adjust your goal and aim for something different. Whatever your response to obstacles, it is always most effective if identified and prepared for in advance. Reaction is hardly ever as effective as preparation when it comes to making a change.

What is most important in removing obstacles is not just listing them; you must categorize them to make them workable. You will find there are three types of obstacles—ones we can control, ones we cannot control but can influence, and ones that are out of our control. For instance, if your goal is to get a better job, obstacles could include finding the time to get to interviews or improve your credentials by taking on courses. Family commitments or the demands of a personal relationship might also make it difficult to put in extra hours in the office or take the extra time away from home to pursue the opportunities you want.

As you list them, you would find that some fall into the category you may not be able to directly control. These could include such things as the pool of those competing for the same job spot. The ones you could control would be your poor interviewing skills, or lack of effort locating the right kinds of companies to interview with for positions.

As you identify obstacles, your focus will be on those that you can control and can influence. So while you can't control the rate of unemployment and the pool of candidates looking for jobs, you can control your interviewing skills. You could hire a coach, take a class, or read about successful approaches.

Obstacles may seem daunting, but with the S.H.I.F.T. Model™, we bring them to light. We catalogue them and then organize them so we can work them into our plan. Remember that the definition of insanity is doing the same thing repeatedly and expecting different results!

Once you are successful in identifying and categorizing obstacles, the third step in the S.H.I.F.T. Model™ is all about understanding how you impact your quest for change. In the third step you will Identify the Human Factor and take into account all the human-related elements in your planning and goal-achievement process.

Among other things, this step looks at behavioral style, how we all tend to take a different approach to problem solving and communication, and how these different approaches can hamper our ability to connect and work together most effectively. The human factor step requires introspection, but it also requires us to look outward to see who else in our universe will have an impact on our decisions. This step looks at the issues you might have within yourself and within your network of relationships. It looks at factors such as toxic friendships or poor self-esteem that might hold you back. Other things, like a supportive spouse or good self-confidence, might give an advantage in a particular area. Basically, it requires you to look at the stakeholders, anyone and everyone with an interest in your life, who therefore can influence — for better or for worse — any change process you are looking to pursue.

Once the first three steps are completed, the model moves to Finding Alternatives. The fourth step essentially acknowledges what Robert Burns said (and what John Steinbeck noticed), that the best-laid plans "of mice and men" do not often work out. You strive toward your desired outcome, but I also believe in always having a "Plan B"! It is generally part of making any effective shift — for both planning and execution — to have alternative routes in place.

Finding alternatives can be fun, though, and it often allows creativity to flow. To make the process practical and workable, take this step only after other steps have been completed. It is hard to know what options you have until you have clearly specified your goal, your obstacles, and the human factors you will encounter in your change process.

The last step in the S.H.I.F.T. Model™ is to Take Disciplined Action, and it is with this step that you get to create your specific plan in a methodical fashion, possibly also identifying and incorporating back-up plans as well.

This last step sets out to change the too-common dynamic of having an idea, talking about it, planning for it, and thinking about it for a long time, only to never actually do anything! There's no substitute for working to turn this idea into an actual, valuable shift for you.

Using this last step, you can set out knowing that you are aware of what you need to do. With this information you can also confidently construct a very clear plan to get you where you want to be. In a kind of business sense, this is where skills like project-management skills, time-management skills, and resource-management skills come into play. In other words, this is the point at which you need to start thinking about your shift as a strategic exercise.

As you work your way through this book, working on each of these steps, keep in mind that individuals and businesses have been using the S.H.I.F.T. Model™ in their work with me for years. They've used it without knowing what it was called, without necessarily knowing the names of each individual step. The point is to look beyond the nametags, beyond the basics of each step, and see what it is that the step sets out to achieve.

The S.H.I.F.T. Model™ is a process that works if you are prepared to recognize the fundamental principles within. Let's get started!

"It is never too late to be what you might have been."

— *George Eliot*

CHAPTER 1

Specify Your Desired Outcome

As human beings, we really are goal-seeking even when the goal isn't good for us! To get truly motivated and to stay motivated, we must focus on an end goal that is meaningful to us. Much of the time, though, we have an "I should" goal, or a long-term goal that's hard to believe in. You know you need to define where you are going before you can make a meaningful journey. But how do we figure out what is meaningful to us? You do not have to know much about life or even individuals to reckon that most of us have very little idea about our true passions or what will make us happy. Think of all those classic romance novels in which the hero or heroine is blissfully unaware of the person in their life that is destined to make them happy. In most instances, they are unaware right up until the final scenes. And art, as they say, imitates life.

Why Does What Matters, Matter?

Why is figuring out what really matters so hard for us? It is because often we are moving away from something we do not like instead of moving toward something we do want. Couple this with the fact that we do not take into account all of the factors of who we are, and it can be a recipe for disaster when we do get what we want. Where did the adage "Be careful what you wish for!" actually come from? Someone getting what they thought they wanted and finding out that "Oh-oh—this isn't it!"

For example, it is not enough to hate your 9-5 job and decide to start a home-based business. You could set your SMART goal about this, but (among many other things) you can't actually go into business without knowing what business you want to be in. You have to know what skills you have, what impact it will have on your family, etc. Similarly, if you set a goal of "Obtaining a college degree," you wouldn't want to complete a college education without knowing what degree you were going to receive and why you wanted that particular degree.

We do not do many things in life without having some sense of why we are doing them, but we rarely think deeply or even the right way about why we are doing those things.

It doesn't mean we do not think about the future. It doesn't mean that we never take action in pursuit of our goals. Of course we check the list and do many things that are meaningful to us. We might take the class, or make a New Year's resolution to identify what we hope to accomplish over the next year. It is taking the time to create our vision of success—to be clear about the desired outcome we have for change—that we put off or never do. When it comes to many of the things that matter the most, we just do not take the time to paint a picture of what we really want out of the experience.

For instance, maybe you aren't trying to flee a bad boss or difficult work environment. Your goal to have your own business is really to have more time to spend with family. You are still going to fail in your shift if you set up a business, however much of a profit it generates, that allows you to spend very little time with family. You might have more time with family, but what if you aren't making enough to make the ends meet? You have overlooked the work you want to do, or the profitability equation. You will not sustain the shift as long as you think. At the very least, you probably won't feel all that much happier than you did before.

Cause and Effect

We tend not to look too closely at what I call "cause and effect." For example, if I set a goal that says, "I want to make a million dollars this year," is that really the sum and substance of my life? What if I have an elderly mother who needs my attention? What if I want to engage in charitable endeavors this year? What other aspects of my life are important to me? If I state my overall goal of a million dollars, I may reach that goal but I may sacrifice other things that were important to me. I may end up with a million dollars, but if I'm working 100-hour weeks and have not seen my ailing mother once, have I really achieved all my goals?

If I state my overall goal only in the quantitative terms I am striving for, I miss out on other aspects of what kind of life I want to have, and how I want to be known to the people around me. I have observed this repeatedly with my hypnotherapy clients. We might write a goal, but once that exact goal is attained, there is the feeling of "something is missing" or "what happens next?"

It is not enough to decide you want to start your own business, to say that you want to lose weight, make more money at your job, or go back to college. You need to know exactly what you want to do, what type of business you want to set up and why, how much weight you want to lose, what kind of job you want with what kind of conditions, or what you want to study at college and—most importantly — why these goals matter to you.

Ask "Why?"

Depending on the "why" of your goal, how you construct your desired outcome will go deeper than merely goal setting. More than this, though, you will be able to look at your goals with a broader view, seeing the longer-term benefits and sacrifices, understanding the values that are underlying your goal and how you can incorporate them into your life most effectively.

Consider this scenario. Your goal is to lose 10 pounds because you'd like to achieve a healthier body mass index (BMI) and you also have a history of high cholesterol in your family, to which you would be less susceptible if you controlled your weight and developed a healthier lifestyle.

Even without considering the second factor here, the goal of achieving a healthier BMI suggests an emphasis on achieving a healthier lifestyle, rather than just simply losing weight for the sake of fitting into a smaller size. An emphasis then, in pursuing this goal, should be to develop a healthier lifestyle and a sustainable one. Knowing this, you can weed out the number of possible, practical dieting options and exercise plans. If the goal is really to lose weight to be healthier, then the real desired outcome is a healthier lifestyle along with the 10 pounds lost. You need to create a program for change that is all about shifts that can be sustained. In other words, not crash diets but healthier food choices that, in the long run, help you to get to a healthier weight. You can also assume that you're not really looking to just lose a certain amount of weight and go back to the eating and activities you were doing beforehand. You could, but you would probably still feel that you had to make a substantial shift in this area of your life.

What, then, about starting a business? Unless you have virtually unlimited resources, you can't just wake up one morning and pull a business idea out of a hat, deciding to take it upon yourself to start that type of business for yourself. You need to think carefully about the type of business that is right for you, even, perhaps especially, if you are the only person who is going to be involved in it on a daily basis. You have to ask yourself: Why am I really interested in setting up my own business? After all, it is a lot of work, it takes a considerable amount of discipline, it can be very stressful. What are the desired outcomes? What do you see as possible benefits of your own business that justify the effort? Perhaps more time at home, more flexible work schedules? Maybe you are more passionate about your own business idea than you ever could be about working in a traditional 9-to-5 job, and you see your own business as a way to be happy.

Finally, let's consider the college example, because it is definitely an issue that many people struggle with at various stages of their lives. What if going to college or going back to college is your goal? What is the problem with just having this as your goal?

Well, first, you can't even apply to most colleges without some notion of what you want to study. Sure, you do not have to declare your major. To get through the application process, though, you are bound to have a problem if you can't register interest in a specific type of degree and indicate the general subject you are interested in. At the very least, you have to look at what you want to do with the degree once you have it. What are the underlying desired outcomes of this decision to go to college?

Say you want to go to college to get a better job. From a goal-setting perspective, you have to think about your desired outcome in detail. What type of job do you want to have with this degree that you cannot have without it? The answer to this question is going to have a major impact on your choice of degree and the subject. What degree program is going to be most practical, most helpful, to your longer-term desires? How many people come out of school holding a degree in something they were passionate about at the time, but never felt fulfilled by as a profitable job?

Capturing desired outcomes using the S.H.I.F.T. Model™ approach means looking at your objectives and goals in a rather holistic way. It asks you to consider the context of your life, your values and long-term preferences. When a goal is more traditionally set in a vacuum, it is likely that the goal will be met and something else may be sacrificed in the process.

One Thing Impacts Another

To illustrate how the traditional goal-setting process can actually hamper our efforts, I'll share a personal story in the development of my career. I had previously been taught to look at the different segments of my life—work, family, spiritual, hobbies, etc.—and to set goals for each one individually (using the SMART process, of course). Before I fully grasped the importance of clearly defining what success meant to me by looking at its overall impact on my life, I made the mistake of taking steps in a particular direction. I focused on one goal, without realizing how one area actually blended into another. In this example, I wanted to be a popular public speaker, and I set a goal of being well paid to speak all across the country on topics that I really enjoyed. When I set this goal, however, I didn't think about the impact it would have on my family. I didn't think about how much I would miss my children, or about the physical wear and tear I'd have to endure, traveling around the country. I found myself being wildly successful and in demand all over the country, getting paid to speak in many different forums on topics I enjoyed. So, I reached the goal I had set and technically, I should have been happy as a result. But I realized that I couldn't fully enjoy my success since I also gave up so much, because I didn't take the time to clearly define my desired overall outcome for my life and establish what success would mean to me in that context. I did not even think about why I wanted this goal. If I had looked at my overall desired outcome, and all of the components of who I am and what matters to me, I would have realized I was missing key aspects of my definition of "success."

This is not an uncommon situation. People often get fixated on a goal, or focus on one thing that they dream of and desire. But my own experience, and those I see from working with individuals and businesses, have taught me that it is important to look at the whole picture and understand exactly what we want—and why we want it. The problem with classic goal setting, as most of us have come to understand it, is that the goals tend to be formulated in a vacuum. We have a desire, we set the goal, and then we put steps in place in order to help us meet that goal. But as humans we are more complicated than this, and as businesses we have a variety of dynamics that are at play each and every day. To simply set goals that say "I will do this" or "We need to reach that objective" is missing a large piece of the overall puzzle. We do not think about the "why" even though we have a variety of dynamics that are at play each day. Even when we go through the motions of writing out some kind of formal plan for our goals and we try to set SMART goals, because we follow the same process to pick our goals, we end up with the same problems repeatedly.

Did I Want This?

One client I worked with recently had finally achieved her long-held goal of running a charitable organization. She was a very goal-oriented individual and felt she "should be happy" with what she had achieved. But when I went to visit with her for our first meeting, she was feeling defeated and depressed. Although she had met the goal she set, she was miserably unhappy because there were many other factors that she did not take into account when setting her sights on this goal. The role wasn't what she had expected, and the organization wasn't in line with her values and her aspirations. She had reached the point that she just hated getting up in the morning to go to work. But at the same time she was feeling guilty about her feelings, because she had achieved what she had wished for! She was especially unhappy because she thought she should be happy. "This IS what I wanted," she said. But it missed so many important components of what was valuable to her, that it wasn't really what she wanted.

Instead of classic goal setting, we need to paint a picture of what success in its entirety looks like to you. What is your personal desired outcome over the next year or few years? For a business, what does success look like to your firm? What you want to describe is the entire picture of what you care about and how your life will look when you reach the desired outcome you are seeking. We want to think about the different components of who we are and what matters to us. These variables will change based upon the goal we desire. But as an example, if I am thinking of making a career change I might consider:

- Why I want to leave the position I am in — what makes me unhappy here
- The kind of industry I enjoy
- The role I like to play within a company
- The income I need to sustain the lifestyle I desire
- Whether commuting is important to me
- Whether family/life balance is important to me
- What kind of culture I thrive within

- When I want to make this move

If I have identified all of these factors, a well-defined desired outcome might be: "To shift my job focus to a new (defined) industry within the next 24 months, where I achieve a role as (defined job), work in a company that is entrepreneurial and exciting to me, and make no less than I am making now. This job will be no more than a 45-minute drive from my home, to allow for work and family balance. I will leave work feeling good about what I am doing each night, and go in each day feeling excited."

When we set goals that say only that we need to reach a particular objective, such as "I want to find a new job," we are missing a large piece of the overall puzzle. Instead of classic goal setting, we need to paint a picture of what success looks like in its entirety. What does success look like to you as a kind of three-dimensional entity? What do you care about, what are your priorities, and what might you be willing to sacrifice in your quest to achieve a specific goal? You can't determine this without identifying first what is most important.

Multiple Facets of Defining the Goal

As we have discussed, our complexity as human beings means we have many aspects to who we are. Why, then, does classic goal setting tell us to categorize the aspects of ourselves and of our lives, setting goals in each category—Financial Goals, Spiritual Goals, Family Goals, etc.?

We know we are complex—often like a Rubik's Cube. It is difficult for most of us to focus on one thing without having an impact on something else. The best goal setting looks at the entire picture at the outset and identifies all of the components of what is most important. You have to see the whole, big picture to solve the puzzle.

In my corporate work, I use an analogy with teams when they are quick to give me answers to a problem. I ask them to think about a Jenga™ tower—the game where you pull out one piece at a time, hoping the whole tower won't come falling down on your turn. This is what scattershot decision-making and having goals in a vacuum can do. You might pull out a piece that makes sense for that one area, but it causes the rest of the tower to fall down. This is what often creates the "fire drill" mentality, both in a business scenario and in personal lives. We fix one thing, only to have to turn our attention to fixing something else. And all this fixing detracts from our time pursuing our passion.

Not looking at how all of the pieces might fit together in our desired outcome can often mean that we get something in place, but then something else falls out of place (like my example of being successful as a speaker, but troubled as a mom by traveling too much).

Looking at your overall desired outcome allows you to take into account all of the pieces that matter to you. You will not want to focus too much on single, specific goals, like the singular focus I illustrated with my client at the charitable organization above. You do want your desired outcome to be a clear and measurable goal. That means statements like "I want to become a nicer person" or "I want to be rich" just do not cut it. We've read stories of the people who made it rich and it ruined their lives, because a singular focus on wealth can sometimes bring unintended consequences. Stories abound of the person who won the lottery, only to determine they would like to give it back because of the headaches it created!

Looking at your overall desired outcome asks you to take into account all of the pieces that matter to you. You have to think about what you want your life to look like once you have made your shift and achieved the goals you are striving toward.

And at this stage, you certainly want to identify single, specific goals, but you also want your final desired outcome to be a comprehensive, clear, and understandable overall definition of what success looks like to you—and perhaps to the people who are close to you, as well.

The Why Behind the What

Before you begin to record your desired outcome, think about what matters to you. For example, if you picked up this book because you want to lose weight, ask yourself why you want to lose weight. Is it to look good in a bathing suit? To know that you are getting healthier? To get into clothes that now hang in your closet unworn? Think about why you want to set any goal you have. What is the real reason for what you are trying to do? It would have been beneficial for my client to ask why she wanted to work for that charitable organization. Her passion was to help people, and identifying this would have helped to put a focus on the culture within the organization. Not all charitable endeavors have staff members focused on "helping"! Every time we have a desire, something we wish to do, there is an underlying "why" behind it.

In a more positive example in my own life, I wanted to write a book in 2009. With my three youngish children, a houseful of pets, a husband, and a very demanding consulting business, it seemed like a far-fetched goal to set. But I knew how much I wanted to do it. And the reason was that I felt a responsibility to get information out to people who were struggling in their relationships. I didn't particularly care about making money from the book. I didn't care about receiving accolades or recognition. I just wanted the chance to do something that might be helpful to others. My desired outcome looked like this: "This year I will finish a book to help others communicate more effectively. I'll find the time to do this without detriment to my family or my business. The book will allow people a chance to learn how to better understand themselves and get along with others."

There were a few components to my desired outcome. After learning from my mistake of focusing solely on being a public speaker, I knew I did not want to write this book if it meant too much time and distraction away from my family or my successful business. So I was faced with the reality that my desired outcome required using time that I didn't really have, given other demands on me at that time. By having a clear view of this outcome and by taking into account all of the important elements of my life, I somehow found the time and focus to be able to write the book and reach my desired outcome that year. Coincidentally, and as an aside, I was also able to write two more books in the same year for the industry I focus on in my consulting business, and one of those books was reviewed and recommended to its members by one of the major industry resource groups. Using this proven process on my own situation, I somehow found the ability to write not one book, but three!

To set a desired outcome, first think about what is creating your desire to make a shift in your life. What is your "why?" Do you feel out of place in the career you have chosen? Are you missing out on time with your family and your children? Are you tired of being tired and feeling out of shape? Are you addicted to a certain drug or food that seems to control your life? Record what triggered you to consider reading this book — what is happening that prompts you to want to make a shift.

As part of that process, think about your situation if you do not make a shift. Where will you be if things do not change for you, and you do not make any movement at all toward your desired outcome? Thinking of this helps us more fully understand the why of what we want to do and helps us to clarify where we need to shift.

Worksheet 1: Specify Your Outcome

What is prompting me to seek this goal/desired outcome?

Why do I care so much now about reaching this goal?

What would happen if I didn't care about this goal?

Moving Toward? Or Away From?

Once you know where you are and what has triggered your goal, you can start to create a scenario of where you want to be. So, for example, let's say you're tired of working in a corporate setting and you want to launch your own business. A typical goal would be "I want to start my own business." But it is important to be much more specific, and clearer about the desired outcome. Why do you want to start your own business? What benefit will accrue to you by doing so? What will happen to you if you do not start this business? Why do you see this as important? Is it because you want freedom? Is it because you want more money? A more relaxed lifestyle? Pride of ownership? To get away from a terrible boss?

There are two basic reasons we move in a new direction: to move toward something new and positive, or to move away from something that we dislike. Both are motivators and both will urge us to action. When we are moving away from something, we had better have a clear view of what comes next. What is the outcome we hope for when we get where we want to go? This is important because oftentimes people leave situations or move away from something they do not like, but end up no better in the new place. This is typically why many second marriages have a higher divorce rate—I moved away from the first person but, whoops, I didn't figure out enough about where I went next! Consider what is motivating you—dig down to uncover the reasons behind your desire to shift to this goal.

Once you have identified what is driving the goal, you can begin to clarify the desired outcome. As you come to understand what is creating the desire for the shift, you may uncover more specifics about what is important to you. Instead of "start my own business," you might have revised your goal to something like: "Find something I enjoy doing that I can make a business out of where I work from home three days a week and have more time to spend with my family." Or alternatively: "Launch and run a successful business doing something I truly enjoy doing and from which I am able to make $50,000 per year."

Maybe your initial goal to start your own business had to do with the freedom of working without a boss (this is an example of an "away from" type of goal—"no more difficult bosses for me!"). But you may find that the real objectives are more about finding something you enjoy doing, making a living at it, and having time to spend with your family (this is an example of a "moving toward something" goal—"a positive outcome for me in my life overall").

Having a bad boss may have precipitated your desire to shift, but maybe it wasn't the real reason you decided to pursue the change. Shifting to get away from the boss—a mistake many people make in career change or leaving a position—doesn't mean you will end up somewhere better. Again, wise adages exist for a reason—the grass is not always greener. And I've watched many people run away from a situation rather than toward something else they want.

Once you look at all of the pieces, and can create a clear and multi-faceted scenario like this with a lot more detail to illustrate what is important to you, you can navigate with more confidence toward what you want. Writing the entire scenario as the desired outcome has now become a first step. As you move toward your shift, you will be able to check in with your desired outcome to make sure that where you are headed includes all the different components of what is important to you.

Solve the Right Problem

Understanding the "why" behind what we want can help us to more deeply crystallize what it is we're really after. There is no more powerful question than "Why?" Before you firmly set your goal, it may be necessary, and it is certainly important, to do a bit of soul searching. If you have not done it already, find out what is really driving your desire for change.

Once I was going through this process with a client, and I kept asking for more clarification on the desired outcome. She finally turned to me and asked, "So you really want me to solve the right problem instead of just the problem I think is most important to me?" And that about summed it up—we can spend a lot of time and energy trying to get somewhere, but unless we're very careful in analyzing where we want to go, we might arrive at the place we set out for and realize it isn't where we want to be at all, and that it doesn't really shift us from our current state in a real and lasting way.

Let's consider a goal of going back to college as an adult. If you consider the common motivating factors of this decision, you'll notice that many people are not only looking to improve their credentials so that they can, at some point, get a better job; they are also looking to boost their self-confidence and enhance their knowledge and learning, which, in itself, is often very satisfying. Thinking about these other, intangible aspects might influence what kind of degree is right for me. I might pursue a track that I feel good about and enjoy and where I also can make a living. As a college professor, it often pains me to see how many students are just going to "get through." Why not find ways to enjoy the process, too? I watched my father, like many people, get the degree he "should" have and then spend his career in a job that made him miserable. Once he finally quit and did something totally unrelated, but that he was passionate about, his experience of working changed completely.

Think about it—if you focus on choosing a degree that will simply get you a better job, you might miss out on doing something else that would be ultimately more rewarding. And in an ironic twist, doing what you love might lead to a better job down the road!

Now, of course, the things that matter to us do change over time, but we need to take into account everything that currently matters to us when we are hoping to move to a new place. To simply "trade" one important priority for another rarely brings us the overall success for our firm or the happiness we are hoping to achieve. I was always very career-oriented with no desired outcome to have children, but they showed up anyway! Once they did, my desired outcome shifted completely. They are the biggest blessings I could ever imagine, and so they became the center around which I make most of my decisions. As we look at where we are going, we can only work with the information we have at the time — so if you have made decisions that you wish you could undo, either undo them or accept them and move forward from where you are now.

Consider All Aspects

A broader perspective allows you to keep more than one thing in front of you as you forge toward a goal. Think of it as incorporating both quantitative and qualitative aspects into your goal, into identifying the desired outcome and seeing how it fits in your life.

A blueprint to use, when trying to scope out what you want your life to look like after a shift, is to consider your objectives or desires in each of the following areas:

In Your Personal Life — whether you're single, in a relationship, or married (or anywhere in between), what are your goals for your personal life and how do other people factor into this goal? What kind of life do you want to have as the person you are or in conjunction with the people around you? What matters most to you — what do you most care about?

In Your Family Life — However you may feel about them, your family is often your strongest link to the past and the group of people most likely to be there for you in the future. To be grounded and confident in yourself (and thus better able to pursue your goals), it helps to know where you're coming from. That's your family. How do they fit into your desired outcome? How is your relationship to them, the time you spend with them, going to be affected by your planned shift? How are you going to feel about any changes to your relationship and time spent together, if any? This can pertain to your current family and also your family of origin. We will talk more about these people aspects in the human factor step, too.

In Your Career — We may sit with a guidance counselor to identify our career objectives in order to choose the appropriate college. As we go off into the world, how often do we get side-tracked when it comes to our career goals? If you have some aspect of your professional life that you have not addressed in a while, some personal goal for a career that you have not achieved, factor this into your goal setting. What are you good at? What do you love to do and why do you love it? What makes you happy from a working perspective?

In Your Intellectual Development — Knowledge is food for the mind as spirituality is good for the soul. You do not have to be a straight-A student to enjoy learning new things, particularly when you're an adult. You do not have to take a course to develop your intellect, either. You could simply join your local library and commit to reading one book a month or every two weeks, depending on what your schedule allows. You do not necessarily have to do anything, but if you like to have time to yourself to read or to have the opportunity every now and then to learn something new, consider the impact of your goal on this.

In Terms of Your Physical Well-Being — Everyone needs time to burn off steam or, on the other hand, to be decidedly still and re-laxed. Consider the impact your goal may have on your physical and mental well-being. For instance, if you are going back to college and studying long hours, how might this impact your diet and workout habits? How will this change affect you?

Doing Good Work for Others—For many people being able to give back, or contribute somehow, is very important. Does this matter to you? If so, why? What do you want to be able to do in this regard? What kinds of things make you happy about giving or contributing?

Spiritual or Religious—Many people care deeply about some-thing bigger than they are. This could manifest in your own reli-gious affiliation or simply the desire to be closer to a Higher Power. What does this quest look like for you? Does it matter at all? How do you want it to be included in your overall desired outcome?

Stating your desired outcome clearly is the first step to achieving your goals, but the second step is to realize that there are many ways to do things. What is important is that you establish a plan to achieve your goals that includes all of the aspects that are important to you and then state your desired outcome, including everything you need to achieve—without sacrificing one goal for another.

Put it in Writing!

Taking the time and being crystal clear in identifying, in writing, your desired outcome keeps you on track once you finally create your plan (the last step in the S.H.I.F.T. Model™). Have you ever set out to do something and then found you were wasting time on something else? You might have been frustrated and wanting to turn your attention back to your important goal, but you were so engaged in the other thing that you couldn't do it! I've found this to happen with many of the executives that I coach. We may start the week out with a clear set of desired outcomes, but then when we time-track at the end of the week, the time has been spent in other areas. When that happens, I need to ask them, "Is this objective really that important to you?" Things that aren't really priorities and that won't lead to the ultimate goal will end up getting in the way, and the person I am working with may start to feel frustrated that they have not made the progress they desire.

Having a clearly defined (and written!) set of success objectives for yourself can help you decide what you should spend time on. After all, it is easy to get distracted and spend your time and energy on things that aren't really high-gain activities. Think about how we can get distracted just sitting at a desk; by reading funny emails, or by visiting a social media site, or by chatting on the phone with someone for a long period of time. At home there is also an endless range of distractions, from household chores to the people and pets that might live with you and make demands on your time.

When I recently set a desired outcome that was a very important spiritual one for me, I had to consider all of the other time demands I had. It involved, in my case, bringing God into my daily activities and making Him a part of what I was doing. For me, it was not about going to church or doing good deeds. It was about feeling as if I had a relationship and could focus on Him on a more regular basis. I had always carved the time out separately, and now my desired outcome was more about integration into day-to-day living. This completely changed my way of thinking about something that had been elusive to me in the past. I restated a desired outcome, taking into account how my life worked and what was doable and reasonable. Meditating for an hour each morning, counting on prayer time during my walk with my rambunctious dogs, or going on spiritual retreats just wasn't going to cut it! I had to create a desired outcome—yes, even for God—that considered how my life actually works.

As with all desired outcomes, I have to keep bringing my focus back to what I want. Our life is all about distraction, and if I am not clear in the outcome that matters to me, it is too easy to find other things to focus on. Wait—what was that email about? What a laugh—I need to scroll through my mail list and find 50 people to send it to.... And this is how it goes all day. Fundamentally, if we want to make our personal shift, it is a matter of keeping all the pieces in place and not trading one for another. Keeping focused on your desired outcome actually makes your life a bit easier. I can catch myself and ask, "Does this move me closer to this goal?" The question is no longer a broad-based question of what you should be doing; now it is a question of what will move you closer to your goal most efficiently. It gets easier to say "no" to distractions or things that do not matter as much.

As you have read this chapter, have you had a chance to think more clearly about what you are really looking for in your shift? Before you move on to the next step, take the time to record your desired outcome in its entirety—the place you want to shift to in your life, or in a particular area of your life. These can be smaller goals like spending more time with your kids or with your significant other, or they can be much larger objectives around shifting to become a business owner or shifting to a new job, making or having more money, losing weight, living healthier, or going back to college.

Be sure to reflect back to when you stated the "why" of this goal and what matters to you about it now.

- What is the desired outcome?

- How do I define success? (here paint the picture in as much description as possible)
- What are the quantifiable (measurable) aspects of the goal?
- What are the qualitative aspects of the goal?
- When do I expect (or need) to meet this goal?
- What do I not want to sacrifice in meeting this goal?

The SMART Goal-Setting Process

You may still be having a hard time understanding all of the ways to think about your desired outcome. If so, try jogging your thinking by using SMART goal setting, as we mentioned a bit earlier. By itself, the SMART approach to goal setting, while widely used, is often not enough. SMART goals, however, are worth using as part of a more comprehensive approach. The approach was invented by George Doran, Arthur Miller, and James Cunningham, who wrote an article about goal setting in 1981. This well-known approach to arriving at a goal is taught in many colleges and used by many businesses, and I use it in the Leadership course I teach to illustrate how to break down a goal when someone is struggling to fully define their desired outcome.

Again, the five SMART criteria are that the goal must be specific, measurable, actionable, realistic, and time-bound. You may want to go back and review your desired outcome and make sure it is specified clearly in terms of an overall desired outcome, and not just a simply-stated goal. See if it is measurable. If you look back at the examples in this chapter, you'll find that there are almost always numeric and quantitative components that can be measured. If there aren't measurements built in, it may be hard to know if you have reached the success you desired. "Actionable" and "realistic" means that you know what you need to do to get the goal accomplished, and that it is a feasible goal. For example, if you are currently breaking even with your business and you set a desired outcome to make a million dollars next year, it might not be a very realistic goal given other factors in your job or your knowledge of investing. Finally, time-bound means defining when you want to reach this goal. "Losing weight at some point" could mean next month or it could mean 15 years from now, and it is crucial to know which. I have seen many individuals and businesses set the same goal year after year because they have not identified a specific point in time—a certain date—they want to accomplish something. We'll take a closer look at this when we get to the last step: taking disciplined action and identifying how you will actually accomplish your shift—the what, the when, the who in detail for your plan.

Before you read on, take the time to use the worksheet on page 29 and capture what your desired outcome entails, why it is important to you, and what quantifiable and qualitative measures you will use to know when you have achieved it.

"The truth is that our finest moments are most likely to occur when we are feeling deeply uncomfortable, unhappy, or unfulfilled. For it is only in such moments, propelled by our discomfort, that we are likely to step out of our ruts and start searching for different ways or truer answers."

—*Unknown*

CHAPTER 2

Highlight and Categorize Your Obstacles

In the S.H.I.F.T. Model™ each step is important, but the second step often makes the difference, determining whether an individual or organization keeps doing the same thing repeatedly or has a breakthrough about what they need to do differently.

Most of us have heard the definition of "insanity"—doing the same thing over and over again but expecting a different result. But even though we intuitively understand the insanity, we stay insane too much of the time. For instance, we have the same fights with people, we engage in the same futile activities, we put the same ineffective plans into place, but somehow we think that this time we'll get a different outcome from using the same approach. Then, of course, we are disappointed with ourselves and with our results because, yet again, something didn't work.

During the holidays I am often interviewed about how people can get along more effectively with those family members they simply can't stand. It is always funny to me, because the beauty is that we know these people will do their thing! They have not changed since the last holiday gathering, most likely. So why do we not make a plan for how we will deal with them? Why do we just hope they will have changed their evil ways? We know certain obstacles are there and we know some will enter our path. I love knowing my obstacles — it gives me the power to do something about them where I can, and stop wasting time over those I can't control. We set out with the best of intentions, only to be thwarted by some unforeseen (or foreseen) obstacle in the way. Yes, the realities of life will kick in for each of us on our way to our goals, but if we have not identified those realities we are not giving ourselves a chance to succeed.

What Stands in the Way?

Obstacles are those things that stand in our way — the problems, the issues, the difficulties we've already had, or may at some point encounter. Highlighting obstacles can be difficult, because most people do not like to be complainers and they often do not want to focus on what is, or might be, a problem somehow. In my corporate experience, many organizations do not want to "open a can of worms" by asking their staff what is working and what is not.

The person who is an optimist will say, "Why look at the problems? We'll just forge through and figure it out as we go along!" while the pessimist might say, "Once I realize how much is in my way, I lose my motivation to do anything!"

Both sides are missing an important part of the equation. In my dealings with people, I have lost count of the number of people who are reluctant to talk about obstacles. "I do not want to be a complainer," said a client of mine this week. She said, "Why should I talk about what is wrong in my life — what I want to know is how to fix things!" I often hear from the leaders of groups or companies that we deal with, "Do not bring me a problem — bring me a solution!"

What most people misunderstand in this situation, though, is the importance of identifying those things that may block the successful accomplishment of the desired outcome. Once identified, it is possible to create a plan that manages around, or eliminates, these obstacles. It is the only way to turn obstacles into opportunities. Just pretending they do not exist does not make them go away. We always have the option to use a reframing technique. This is where we might look at an obstacle — say it is my negative Aunt Belle, who always brings me down. I could choose to put a different frame around the way I think about Aunt Belle and see her as a troubled woman needing attention. It is Aunt Belle's problem, not mine. This actually works great — if you can and are willing to do it. If you cannot successfully reframe and Aunt Belle continues to be your problem, then note Aunt Belle as your obstacle and create a plan to get your power back when she stands in your way!

As a simple example to illustrate the importance of this: Imagine that you need to raise money for a charity you care about. You set out with a deadline: You need to have the money by the end of the month, in four weeks. You think about how much you need to save, perhaps how much extra time you need to put in at work, that sort of thing. This is your stated desired outcome and you have identified the amount, the timeframe, and the need.

Unfortunately, if this is all you have considered, you might be due for some unhappy news. One obstacle could be a large credit card bill that is due during this timeframe. Another could be that they are cutting your hours at work this month and you may not get your standard pay. An obstacle could be that your spouse doesn't agree that money should be spent here (this is also a human factor, which we'll address later). Knowing these obstacles and bringing them to light helps you to consider a plan to get to this goal that is realistic, given what you are up against. It isn't meant to dissuade you from the goal (although sometimes, given our obstacles, we do need to revise our desired outcome), but it is meant to help you highlight them to plan around them. Who likes negative surprises? No one that I have ever met! So do not set yourself up for failure—figure out what stands in the way. Many times clients express surprise that their well-laid plans have gone awry, when all they really needed to do was spend some time identifying obstacles and considering them in planning.

Capture All Obstacles

It can actually be fun and somewhat cathartic to have a legitimate reason for capturing our obstacles. Let's look at our going-back-to-school example. If your desired outcome is "to obtain an MBA in the next five years so that I can apply for jobs inside of my company that require an advanced degree," some of your obstacles might be as follows:

1. Time to take classes is limited—already working 55-hour weeks and not spending enough time with family.
2. Limited money to take classes—company will only pay for two classes per semester and only if you maintain a "B" average.
3. When you were in college you hated to study—you were a procrastinator.
4. There are no schools near your home or office—the closest school is a 45-minute drive, which adds more time to your already overbooked day.
5. Other people within the company have MBAs but have not been promoted—not sure if it is definitely where you want to go.

This list could be longer, of course, but these are examples of real or potential obstacles. The point of this exercise is not to claim that the desired outcome is not possible and you're doomed to stay in your lowly position forever. That's the last thing I would be trying to communicate in a book about getting the success you desire and deserve! The point is that without identifying what we may have run into in the past, and without knowing what we may run into in the future, there is no way to put together an accurate plan that allows us to work around, or completely remove, the obstacles to our success.

While obstacles are things that often stand in our way and prevent us from moving forward, when we recognize what they are and understand them, they can actually give us information about what we need to do to move forward. I sometimes change the word "obstacles" to "opportunities," because doing so shifts my approach to them. Reframing obstacles into opportunities doesn't always work, because they are real issues. I think of the opportunity part in terms of knowing what might stand in the way and being able to see the potential pitfalls in black and white. This actually gives you the guidance you need to create a plan that either removes or plans around these obstacles. Granted, the obstacles you face may be significant ones—health issues, financial issues, family issues, and so on. But it is critical to bring them to light even if they can't be turned into opportunities. No matter what, finding solutions and making plans becomes easier, not harder, when you know what you might be up against.

Better yet, while obstacles often stand in our way and prevent us from moving forward, when we recognize what they are and understand them, they can actually give us information about what we need to break through them.

Capture, then Categorize

Never stop at simply listing your obstacles. Listing them can leave you feeling daunted by the potential trouble you will face trying to overcome them. In fact, if you just stopped at listing expected problems and left it at that, you'd probably have a hard time getting up the next morning! Why bother getting out of bed when there are so many things that might stop you dead in your tracks?

The critical next step, after identifying obstacles, is to categorize them. Organize them into one of three categories: (1) those within your control, (2) those you cannot control but can influence, and (3) those you cannot control.

In this example, you cannot control the fact that your company offers limited money to take two classes each semester. You can control the need to maintain a "B" average, however. The fact that there are no campuses close by is technically out of your control, but you could influence it by deciding to take online courses or move. Though you may not want to admit it, you can influence the fact that you are a procrastinator when it comes to studying, even if it is just by being self-aware of your Achilles heel. The "others with MBAs in the firm not receiving a promotion" obstacle seems out of your control. But influence would include finding out more by speaking with the HR director about what you can do to move ahead.

I have gone through this discovery process with many people and have watched the same scenario unfold many times. The effort starts with my client trying to convince me that their "out of my control" problems prevent success. Yet each time, when we list all of the obstacles (and often there are many) and then go through the categorization process, we find that many of the obstacles are in their control after all, or at least within their influence. In life, there are really few obstacles we encounter that are completely out of our control—they are there and we need to note them, but only so we do not waste our time trying to go through them instead of around them.

Before we discuss identifying your own obstacles, I want to underscore a problem I often see. In general, we tend to waste a lot of time and energy focusing on those few things that we simply cannot change. We rail, complain, and seethe over circumstances and problems that we simply can't solve. I hear individuals complain that they can't reach their goals because something in their history prevents them from doing so, or there's someone in their life who is always setting out to sabotage them: The boss is a problem. The spouse prevents success. The government is unfair. The system is broken, etc. Truth is there are many things that may stand in our way, but to devote our energy to those that we can't change is wasted energy.

In a recent client workshop I did, one of the participants, when asked what he would commit to do differently, raised the fact that he was simply "too busy" to make any changes we had discussed. And yet, this same individual was taking many hours out of his work day to participate in our workshop in the first place! If we value something enough, we'll find a way to work around the obstacle.

In this categorization approach, the people in charge of a company have no control over tax laws, and one's personal history falls into the category of "out of my control" too. So why spend time worrying about either one? In too many cases, energy is spent trying to move things that are actually immovable objects. Trying to move them and wasting time doing so means that a person, or a company, isn't spending that time and energy removing the obstacles they can affect. It is expending resources that could be used in much more productive ways to get stuck on the "can't control" things.

At times, we need to just grumble and complain. I recognize this and when I am coaching, I set a time limit for talking about those out-of-control obstacles. It is okay to vent for a short period, but then we need to move on to look at what can be controlled and influenced. It is very deflating for the person to get fixated on the unfixable!

If you feel stymied about what your obstacles are, answer these questions: "Are you at this desired outcome right now? If not, why not? What is in the way?" Sometimes I ask clients, "Do you go to bed at night feeling great about your life? If not, what stood in your way that day to prevent you from feeling great?" Once you ask these questions, the floodgates usually open and you can discuss obstacles that have held you back.

Whether you realize it or not, you are probably already quite aware of the obstacles you are going to face in pursuit of your goal. You may even have a pretty good handle on the categories they fall into. At this point, the key is to take that awareness and push it just a bit further, so you can work around the obstacles in the future or even turn them into opportunities. You might be saying, "This is stupid. I know what my problems are!" But in order for this process to work well, you need to brainstorm and list the obstacles you encounter to begin this transformation process.

Write It Down!

Start with a blank piece of paper. Look back to your desired outcome, the thing that matters most to you. What has prevented you, or may in the future prevent you, from reaching this goal? Why have you not reached this goal already? What stands in your way?

We all have something that prevents us from doing what we want to do. It can be anything — not enough time, not enough money, lack of knowledge, lack of connections, etc. For instance, many people complain about being too busy and use this as the reason why they do not achieve their goals. H. Jackson Brown, author of the *New York Times* bestseller *Life's Little Instruction Book*, put it best when he said, "Do not say you do not have enough time. You have exactly the same number of hours per day that were given to Helen Keller, Pasteur, Michelangelo, Mother Teresa, Leonardo da Vinci, Thomas Jefferson, and Albert Einstein."

When you capture your obstacles, do not worry at the outset about organizing them—just write them all down. But be sure to be specific. An obstacle like "not enough time" could really be "I'm spending too much time reading books about what I want to do" or "I can't get up early enough in the morning to get a full day out of myself." Let's face it—most of us feel we never have enough time or enough money, but what does this really look like to you? Be as clear as possible about how the obstacle manifests itself in your life.

The degree to which you can make the obstacles specific is the degree to which you will have additional options to solve them. As you list your obstacles, keep asking yourself "What do I mean by this?" and "What is the real issue behind this obstacle?" A way to check yourself on this is to consider whether someone else reading your list could figure out what you mean by what you have written. In other words, do not give it short shrift—be sure you have thoroughly identified and thought through what you mean and why it is an obstacle to you.

Take the time now to brainstorm and identify obstacles that have held you back, or that you fear may hold you back on the way to reaching your desired outcome. Do not judge anything. Just bring them all to the surface.

I've noticed over the years, as I've gone through this process with people, that many times the same underlying obstacle repeats itself with a bit of a different twist. For example, in my hypnotherapy work, if a person isn't meeting their goal of weight loss and I ask them about obstacles, they will respond with "too many cookies in the house," "not enough time to cook good meals," or "too many

Worksheet 2: Identify Obstacles

As I look at the desired outcome, why am I not there today? What is preventing me from reaching this goal?

List the obstacles here:

client dinners." These are all very specific and in the category of "failure to plan." So now I know the overall issue (i.e., lack of planning) and I also know the specifics of how it manifests (i.e., cookies, poor food choices).

Find the Themes

Review your own list of obstacles and see whether you have themes emerging from the obstacles you have identified. Are there things that appear on your list repeatedly but with a slightly different twist? See if you can recognize these and consolidate them before you start to group them. It is very helpful to see our patterns.

The next step is to review your list and organize the obstacles into the three categories: those you can control, those you can't control but can influence, and those that are out of your control. You may need to force yourself out of your comfort zone on this one, as it will come down to how much control you feel you can exercise over different areas of your life.

In one of the college classes I teach, we were going through this exercise. I have two classes back to back, and in both we were talking about the obstacles that might prevent a student from reaching the desired outcome of achieving all "A's."

One of the obstacles was "Having classes I do not enjoy and find difficult to pay attention in." My first class was adamant that this was within the student's control—to prove this, they suggested for example that one could develop a different attitude, one could try and find something good about the course, one could keep focused on their overall goal, etc. On the other hand, my afternoon class was adamant that this particular obstacle was completely out of their control. "If you hate the class, you hate the class" was their general agreement. All of which is to say that the categorization process is a personal one and your ultimate groupings may differ from those of other people. But typically the truly "out of one's control" list is pretty short—most obstacles are either movable or can be influenced in some way.

Review your list and after consolidating similar obstacles, consider where each obstacle fits into the categorization shown on the next page.

Taking this categorizing step can often be the primary catalyst necessary to make change. If I identify obstacles standing in my way and I know which I can control and influence, I can methodically start to put my plan in place. At a minimum, it mentally frees me from the time and frustration I have experienced focusing on obstacles out of my control. It also allows me to see clearly what I can control or influence.

So let's say my goal is to quit my corporate job and move into business for myself. The obstacles might be: I am the major breadwinner in my household; I am unsure of what focus I want my own business to take; my colleagues always tell me how important it is that I work here because of my unique experience; etc. Once I can clearly see these obstacles, instead of feeling threatened by the obstacles or overwhelmed by how much I have to address, my plan for change may actually emerge from looking at the obstacles in black and white and then putting them into the categories. Once I know what I am up against and have a framework in which to view them, I can incorporate steps that will address each one of them as I make my plans to create my personal shift. Identifying obstacles gives us information we didn't consciously have. It highlights ways we have done things in the past that have not worked, factors in our lives we weren't thinking about beforehand, etc. When we know these, we have the opportunity to work with them in an effective way.

Rather than feeling like you have made a list of why you can't, or complaints about what stops you, you may actually find this stage

Worksheet 3: Categorize Obstacles

Obstacles within my control:

Obstacles within my sphere of influence:

Obstacles completely out of my control:

of the process very freeing. Any time we can see things more clearly and have a better understanding of what we are facing, we have more opportunity to put a plan and process in place that's workable! Again, it is a language shift, but if you simply change the words "my obstacles" to "my areas of focus" for those issues that are within your control or within your ability to influence, it opens up channels for creative thinking and changes. Obstacles are oftentimes movable objects and just represent a speed bump in our path, rather than a complete blockage. Creating a plan without identifying obstacles and taking them into account is like diving off a boat in shallow water. Doing so results at best in a headache, and at worst a hospital visit!

Simply seeing the obstacle—that the water is too shallow—allows you to move your boat into deeper waters so you can safely dive and swim. Moving forward without taking the time to identify and categorize your obstacles means you will have to either re-address some or be completely stuck.

"The most basic of all human needs is the
need to understand and be understood."
— Ralph Nichols

CHAPTER 3

Identify the Human Factor

In 2009, I released a book called *Understanding Other People: The Five Secrets to Human Behavior,* which won a Gold Award from Readers Favorite: Book Reviews and Annual Awards. This book was a labor of love for me because of my interest in human behavior. In particular, though, the book gave me an opportunity to consider, in some depth, how people can work and live together more peacefully.

As a certified behavioral specialist and someone who has had the opportunity to observe people interacting in a variety of settings, I believe most problems in life have something to do with the human factor—something that is either within us or within our relationships. In fact, as I travel around talking about how people can build relationships and communicate more effectively, the one common obstacle I find everywhere is having "difficult people" standing in our way.

I've never done a workshop or a talk where I didn't have 100% of the people present raise their hands when asked if they have difficult people who prevent them from achieving their happiness in life. It is a universal experience, and yet probably the most overlooked and undervalued part of any change effort. Ultimately, the human factor will influence whether change comes easily or we fight it all the way.

What is the human factor? In my estimation, it is the combination of internal and external human issues. Internal factors are the ones you bring to the equation; the ones that lurk inside of you for better or for worse. External factors are the other people around you who affect you in some way.

Internal Human Factors

Internal factors are anything you have accumulated throughout your life that either get in your way or help you to succeed. Sometimes the human factor falls under the category we previously talked about as "obstacles." Part of what stands in our way often resides in our human element or the people around us. These include a deeply rooted fear of failure, or as a kid hearing from your parents that "You can't do that—you'll never succeed." Internal factors can be things like a tendency toward procrastination or an unrealistic view of your own abilities. On the positive side of the ledger, the internal human factor could be your resiliency, or a force of will that allows you to plow through situations that someone else may find frightening or worrisome.

Think of the internal human factor as two cartoon beings that sit on each of our shoulders. There is the "good" one, reminding us of our ethics and responsibility, and the "wicked" one, who urges us on to some dastardly deed. We have ways in which our internal self-talk and ways we think help us in our change efforts, and ways in which the negative self-talk or negative ways we think hold us back.

If I have wanted for a long time to lose weight, but my self-control, my fear of being seen in workout clothes, or my fondness for chocolate chip cookies late at night hampers me, then I have just identified aspects of my human factor that are getting in the way of achieving my goal. I might have even captured these things as some of my obstacles, because as you see, the human factor element is often part of our obstacles process.

Conversely, if I want to start my own business and I am comfortable taking risks, creative and resourceful enough, and willing to humble myself to ask for help or support, these aspects of my human factor will be in my favor in the quest for change.

The human factor can pose a problem for you, but it can also represent an advantage and opportunity in your planning process. This is why we look at the human factor separately. Obstacles are problems that stand in the way, but not all human factors are obstacles. Some are very beneficial to us, and we need to identify them and use them as we make our desired shift.

What Holds YOU Back?

If you examine areas where you wish to shift but have not been able to, you will probably find that some internal human factor is holding you back. The ones I hear about most often from individuals have to do with an inability to effectively manage time, a propensity for procrastination, inordinate amounts of unreleased stress or frustration, an inability to control emotions, fear of failure or fear of success, and a lack of clarity about what will really bring about happiness.

These common themes run through many situations. In fact, if someone tells me they have been trying to reach a long-sought-after goal and they find they are unable to make the shift, I ask them about their resistance. What internal human factor is preventing them from being able to free up the energy to SHIFT?

To catalogue the impact of our human factor in our quest to get to our new desired state, we have to be willing to be self-reflective and honest. It is often easy, and all too common, for us to point our finger at the people who are hampering our progress or otherwise getting in our way. When we look inside, many of us have a hard time being honest about how we might help or hamper our own efforts. This isn't meant to be an exercise in bashing ourselves about all we have done wrong or to work through deeply rooted fears; it is merely an exercise in acknowledging their existence and ensuring that our ultimate plan includes a way to deal with the human impact.

Identify and record human factor issues that you know exist, and when you reach the disciplined action stage you will likely find even more that you may not have been aware of. Even though we may desire a change, we are often the saboteurs preventing ourselves from getting to the very change we desire. If we do not acknowledge this, bring it to light, and work with it, it will remain there. It may prevent us from moving past our current state. Before you compile the internal human factors list, it is important to be clear on what is and isn't an internal human factor. Too often people believe that an internal human factor is actually an external human factor. What I mean by this is that we have the human factor that lies inside of us — our own thoughts, feelings, education, behavioral style, values, expertise, and emotions, for example. These things are specific to each of us. Then there are the external human factors, which are all of the people in our lives who may affect our decision to shift in one way or another. These are the people in our lives somehow, but external to us.

In many cases, we'd rather point the finger elsewhere and say that someone or something else is holding us back. It is our spouse, or our kids, or our boss, or our mother, or the local government officials that's the real problem. If not for that person or circumstance, we'd be where we want to be. However, imagine for a moment there is no one else in your life and you are faced with the opportunity to make your shift right now—this very minute. That new job, that weight loss goal, that sales objective, that new job—it is all just sitting there for the taking. What is holding you back from grabbing it with all of your might?

It is What You Say—to Yourself and Others

This is akin to recognizing the Achilles heels in your internal human factor. Instead of denying the negative messages you have heard in your life, wishing they weren't a part of you, recognize that these aspects exist. Acknowledge that they get in your way, so that you won't ignore them. If you have tended to do something that hasn't benefited you in the past, instead of doing it again and again, acknowledge it. Do not just ruminate over it, but make it part of your planning process to address it along with the other steps you will need to take.

Recognize these negative messages and bring them to light. Acknowledging them will generally move them from immovable obstacles to ones you can plan a way to deal with in your process toward shifting. Far too much time is wasted on "what could have been," or "I wish I this," or "If only this person that." Recognize where any of these messages hamper you, if they do.

The problem actually persists if we pretend these internal human factors do not exist or we try to hide them from ourselves. The process of identifying them and acknowledging their existence can oftentimes make them more objective to us—this way, they become a part of our planning process. They can become something we need to consider instead of some kind of problem or weakness that's just there to trip us up.

Maybe your meaningful shift is career-oriented. We often under-estimate the importance of the human factor in the workplace. If you can confront your internal belief system (and possibly help others do the same), you are in a good position to overcome what might very well be some of the biggest obstacles in the workplace. In particular, if you are in a position of authority, you should be ready and willing to challenge your internal belief systems. You need to make sure that you look to yourself first when addressing issues, rather than, possibly, blaming the others in your life. All too often I hear leaders of a firm, or managers, blaming their staff. "They just need to figure it out" is often the refrain. It can be helpful to look at why you believe this. What is stopping you as a leader from investigating more about the true nature of their obstacles? We all need to look at where we resist, blame, or judge, and find out why we do so.

To create a plan that will work for you, one idea is to identify those times when you have actually blamed others and realized later that the problem may really have been about you. Do not be afraid of these times, though — these experiences make up part of who you are, and you can work with them. They have to come into the light so you can raise your awareness and consider them as you make your shift.

One coaching client I had (I'll call him "Harry") kept saying that he would be more effective in his role and take on more risk if only his boss wasn't so angry and verbally abusive. When we explored both internal and external human factors, he admitted that it was really he who deep down did not want to put himself "out there" and make a fool of himself. In our discussions about why this boss affected him so much, Harry disclosed the fact that he had grown up afraid of an angry father. As a child, he had lived lurking in the shadows so as not to face his father's wrath, and the feelings aroused in him by dealing with this boss took him back to his childhood.

Somehow he had transferred these feelings as a little boy with his dad to his boss, and he found himself engaging in similar "hiding" behaviors. It wasn't so much the angry boss as it was a sort of flashback to feelings he had not shed from his boyhood. While our discussions were not of a psychological nature, simply exploring the reaction Harry was having to his boss allowed him to consider why these reactions took root within him. We explored together the "why?" question. Why did his boss bring up these feelings in Harry? As Harry talked about it, he began to see the parallels with his childhood.

As we talked further, Harry also acknowledged that he was not a risk-taker in life in general, and he feared his colleagues and his wife would ridicule him if he went after a position or another level only to fail. He spent a great deal of time talking about his boss, his wife, and how his colleagues would react to him (all examples of perceived external human factors). In reality, as much as he disliked it, he had to admit that his biggest holdback was really him—his own baggage from his past and his current-day concerns about how he might look to the people who mattered to him if he failed. Now I'm not a social worker or a psychologist, but in this case Harry was aware of the deep-seated issues he still had with his dad and he was able to admit his fears around failing. When he expressed to me one day, "I know I shouldn't say this, but I feel like it is my father yelling at me again," I knew that he realized the connection but was uncomfortable talking about it. Some of us do not have the benefit of such self-awareness, or the ability to spend hours with a qualified psychologist. Still, we often recognize certain connections with people or patterns of behavior we have that trace to something we experienced. When we enter a childhood home, interact with a sibling, or have a discussion with a friend from way back, we often feel transported in time! If we are aware of this, we can be aware of the feelings and thoughts these experiences have led to within us.

Once Harry realized and identified what was going on, he was able to create a plan that honored this concern but gave him ways to work effectively with his boss — as his boss and not his pseudo-father. He went after the position and obtained it — with the full support of his wife and his colleagues. He also learned ways to confront his boss professionally. Harry will admit that each day is a work in process, but at least he recognizes the issue for what it is — an internal human factor for him. Now he can continue to deal with it as such. He had to push himself out of his comfort zone to reach his goals, but he found a sense of relief in giving up the blame he had carried around and in feeling as though he was at the mercy of those around him.

Another example of the human factor in action: Dennis became a coaching client about two years after he had retired. He was feeling as if he wasn't contributing anything since he had stopped working, and was experiencing a feeling of hopelessness. At first I was confused about why he came to see me, so it took us a while to define his desired outcome. After working through a few different ideas, he finally stated what success looked like to him: "To get up in the morning twice a week and have a meaningful place to go that feeds my soul and allows me to feel like I am contributing something beneficial."

When we looked at the human factor, we uncovered that Dennis had actually become depressed and unconfident during his two years of not working. He felt so aimless. Instead of realizing that this stemmed from a significant life change, he internalized it and felt himself to be less competent and capable. In addition, his wife and he had fallen into a pattern where she criticized everything he did. So he did nothing — and then she called him "lazy" for not doing anything. We looked at what he could do to improve his own attitude (internal human factor), and how he could collaborate with his wife (external human factor) to find new opportunities.

As they explored different ideas, they found they were not in sync with what was important in retirement. Finally, after several discussions, they settled on something they could agree on — their children. Their daughter had recently moved to a new city and was struggling to fit in. They had both spent a lot of energy in trying to provide her support from afar. Dealing with her issues helped them to realize what a problem this was for people trying to meet others in a new city. They couldn't move to where their daughter was, so instead they became involved with an outreach effort in their own city. They began visiting elderly people who had moved to be closer to their children. Many times these people had left their own roots, friends, and relationships, and were feeling lonely when their children were off living their own lives. Dennis and his wife initially located these people through their church, and then actually worked in a couple of communities advertising what they were doing. They found working together this way to be a fun, "soul nourishing" experience. Dennis would not have been able to create this outcome without identifying his human factors and being honest about them, including his own internal state and the impact his wife was having as a stakeholder in his life.

For many people, the fear of failing or the fear of what people will think holds them back. Fear can prevent you from moving confidently toward a desired shift in a whole variety of situations.

In hypnosis, when someone has a fear, we will go through a process of desensitization where we slowly minimize the person's response to the situation. If I am afraid of flying, I might begin by going somewhere I can hear planes take off and land. I can't see them and I do not need to get on one; I will just listen to the sound. Next I might go to an airport, where I can see planes from afar. Next I will get up close, then step onto a plane that isn't about to take off, and get progressively closer to flying until I finally find myself strapped in and waiting for a real take-off.

Desensitization can be a powerful way to get a person acclimated slowly to an idea or experience they resist. However, for some people desensitization isn't the right way to do things. In a recent article I was reading about new research on overcoming our fears, the author made the case for "admitting to our fears," instead of denying them or trying to overcome them—in other words, the opposite of desensitization where you slowly overcome the fear. According to the author, instead of going into a Zen state to make myself feel comfortable and pretending that I'm not afraid while on a plane 35,000 feet up (which could also be considered avoidance!), I might instead admit, "I am scared of flying, and I'm feeling very uncomfortable right now." The author made the case that instead of working through the fear through a process like desensitization, we should acknowledge the fear but do it anyway! I like this approach, too. It means we bring the fear, or negative internal state, up without judging. We move forward in spite of it and find ways to manage around it.

Now in contrast, you can also use the positive aspects of your human factor to your advantage and recognize where you can leverage them in your shifting process. Be sure you also uncover strengths and attributes you may not be focusing on, or that you may not keep front and center as you shift in new directions. Do you have a core competency that gives you confidence in working toward your goal? Do you have areas of real strength that have served you well in the past? Do you have an inner guide or intuition that tells you what is right for you?

Use the positive aspects of your human factor to your advantage, and recognize where you can leverage them in your shifting process. Are you gregarious and outgoing, and do you get energized being around people? If so, on your path to weight loss you might want to consider joining a class or finding a group of friends to go running with. Are you a confident risk-taker who enjoys proving that you can do something that other people will not? Use this to your advantage as you make your break from a difficult personal or professional situation. Draw upon this as your life or relationship situation shifts to a new place. Keep it in front of you as you confront whatever happens — "I am a risk-taker and I won't shy away from leaving a situation that isn't good for me. I know how to plan and I know what I need to do to reach a desired outcome for my life." Internal human factors include those things that can serve you as you make the process to shift. It is uncovering strengths and attributes you may not be aware of, or that you may not keep front and center as you shift in new directions.

In hypnosis, there is a branch called Neuro-Linguistic Programming. One of the tools for change is to identify a time where you felt good, were successful, or otherwise acted in your personal "zone." If you can capture those feelings, sensations, and experiences, you can transfer them. This is how successful sports figures sometimes compete. If, for example, I know what a great shot feels like to me in my personal zone when I golf, when I get up to tee off I stop for a minute and create this sensation inside of me. We leverage our successful experiences and use them to transfer to something we want to do well in a different area. Understand and then build upon positive aspects of who you are as you move toward new challenges.

It can be helpful to look at experiences in your life where you felt in your personal zone. What did you do? How did you do it? What feelings and thoughts did you have while you were successful? To find your positive internal factors, you might want to reflect back on experiences you'd like to repeat in life and understand why they worked so well!

In step three, you will compile a list of your internal human

Worksheet 4: The Human Factor

What internal human factors (emotions/past experiences/personal beliefs) do I identify as obstacles?

Conversely, what internal human factors might help me make the shift?

factors. Again, it requires some honesty and self-reflection, and it isn't about just finding what holds you back. It is also about identifying factors that will help you to make your shift. Recognizing the positive things that you have to offer can also help you create a more effective and actionable plan. We often fail to unleash the beneficial power we have inside of us.

Use the table to the left to list the internal human factors that come to mind as you think about shifting toward your desired outcome.

Review the two lists you have made. Have you discovered any new obstacles to add to your original obstacles list? If so, go back and add them now.

I have observed that when put into action, the S.H.I.F.T. Model™ is all about leveraging your energy, getting clarity of focus and direction, and using feelings, information, and practical tools to shift confidently in a new direction. For many people, taking the time to lift your internal human factors up, examine them, and understand how you can utilize them, will give you more power as you cross any new threshold.

If You Know It, You Can Fix It!

I was teaching my Leadership class at Suffolk University, where we teach the S.H.I.F.T. Model™, and I asked the students to raise their hands if they found procrastination to be a problem for them. About 75% of the students raised their hands. A little later I asked them how many felt confident they would procrastinate and wait until one to two days before the paper was due to start to working on it. The same 75% raised their hands again. This is a great example of the human factor. If I know I am a procrastinator and can admit to this "failing," why would I set out to do things exactly the same way I always do them? Could it mean that I like the stress, or I do not really want to make a shift in a new direction to make my life easier and perhaps make myself more productive and successful? Is this something I need to work on to make my shift?

If you do want to make your shift, use the opportunity to identify your human factors. After all, if getting to a new and better place is your goal, why not recognize how something may have held you back and resolve to take different steps, or alternatively recognize that something is a strength that can benefit you as you make your shift?

External Human Factors

The external human factors are all of those people who have a say in something you are doing or attempting. Let's refer to them as "stakeholders," because they have a stake in how your shift will eventually turn out. Just as we need to ferret out and examine internal human factors, it is important to recognize the existence of our stakeholders in life. We need to recognize what kind of stake they might have in what we are doing, and use them effectively or plan around them in our quest to shift. We talked earlier about how sometimes we blame others for something that is internal to us. It is also true that other people in our lives can play a role to help us, or thwart us as we make our shift. Our change sometimes threatens others, while some people can be great advocates and give us real help. We need to know who might be involved—for better or for worse—to understand how to consider them as we create our plan for shifting.

Viewing them as stakeholders, there are a few different models that we can use to view them. The most commonly used stakeholder model puts people who have a stake in the change on two scales: power and interest.

A low interest, low power person might be a factor but not someone who requires a lot of your time and energy. In our example,

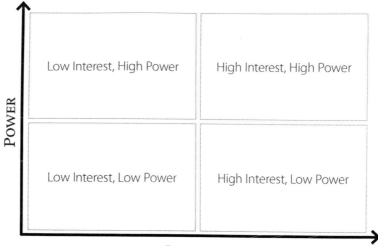

with a quest to lose weight and live a healthy lifestyle, there will be stakeholders for most people. For example, your roommate who doesn't care whether you join the gym or not, but may from time to time park his or her car behind yours when you are hoping to get out for a 6 a.m. cardio class, could be a low/low stakeholder. He or she is still one you want to take into account as you plan your gym schedule—even if it is just to make him or her aware of your plans so your gym days are not the same days their car winds up behind yours. Your boss might be a low interest, high power stakeholder. If your plan to get to the gym involves leaving at 5 p.m. three days a week, your boss could thwart your efforts quite easily with their stake!

In another example, your significant other might be a high inter- est, high power stakeholder as you plan to quit your job and start your own business. If your significant other is actively resistant to the idea and refuses to help you in any way with the financial rami- fications you can expect to encounter in your first years of trying to get the business going, they are a stakeholder with a great deal of control over your destiny and your ability to shift effectively. They will exhibit a high interest in what you are doing and how well it is working, and also a high power in their ability to provide financial and emotional support—or withhold it from you when you most need it.

There are also low power, high interest stakeholders. Your mother, for example, may not be able to help you with the new business but might still want to hear every single thing you are doing. Although she cannot help you materially, she provides a high interest shoulder for you to lean on. High interest, low power people can sometimes be a good sounding board as you make your plans. They have a significant interest, so they care enough to be focused on what you are doing, but they aren't really in a position to control or influence anything for you.

Conversely a high power, low interest person could be your landlord. He or she may have no interest in learning about what you are doing and why, but may exercise his or her power to keep you from running your new business out of your apartment. Like the boss above with the gym example, this is a category we often overlook, because they do not represent a clearly interested party and we do not notice them in our planning process. However, when we are ready to shift, their high power stake could kick in and they could be in a position to either help us significantly or stop us from taking our next steps.

Stakeholders are all around us, and if you ignore their presence at the planning stage they will somehow come into the picture as you make your shift. If they represent an obstacle, you should plan around them. If they are a positive resource, you should leverage their power and interest to help make your shift. Obviously, and depending on the shift you're trying to make, stakeholders may be few or many. If your shift is to become more involved in a local charity by writing press releases and doing public relations work for them, your stakeholders might be limited to your spouse (more time away from the family), the charity you are working with (or at least the contact person there), and the local media whom you will interact with to get publicity. But if your shift involves getting to a new position within your existing company, there may be many stakeholders in the way — your current boss, your future boss, your colleagues, your significant other, your good friend in your current department, the HR representative, etc.

The human factor applies to each of us as individuals as we try to forge our way through change. For the stakeholders in your life, however, resistance to the changes you want to bring about may very well stem from the fact that the new plan doesn't take them into account or doesn't allow them to become invested in your change effort in a positive way. You have to consider the reasons for their resistance.

Recognize the Resistance

Resistance often occurs on a personal level and goes unnoticed. A hypnosis client who wanted to lose weight put all of the right practical steps in place and later was unsuccessful. When we diagnosed her obstacle, we found it to be her husband. She didn't acknowledge him as a stakeholder initially, and so hadn't told him what she was trying to do. He saw what steps she was taking and had started to worry that she was planning to leave him and was "prettying" herself up beforehand! He found many ways to derail her plans to eat healthy foods and get more exercise. Once she realized he was an overlooked stakeholder, she told him what she was trying to do and why. This put his fears at ease, and he actually became a strong advocate for her goal.

Before you can move on to the stage where you brainstorm the options available to you, look again at your desired outcome and the shift you are hoping to make. Think about all of the people who may have some sort of stake in the process—if not now, then at some future point.

Using the worksheet on the next page, brainstorm to identify them and what kind of stake they may hold. Do not worry initially about categorizing; just get all the names and ideas down so you can recognize all of your stakeholders. Remember that the stakeholders in your life are different depending on the shift that needs to happen. It is not a generic list of people who impact your life in some way; it is a list specific to the people who affect your shift process and your goal.

Next, look at this list and put the stakeholders into the traditional interest/power categories. This, again, is the most common grid used to categorize your stakeholders. It does so according to who has either low or high interest, and who has either low or high power.

As with all of the steps, this one will require you to capture what you know now. It is an evolution, and as you begin to develop alternatives (in the next step) you may find there are other obstacles or other human factors that you didn't identify the first time around. The process can't be entirely linear—not many things in life work that way—so it requires you to think as you go through, so that ultimately your plans have considered all of the necessary components for your success.

All of the stakeholders may be important in some way, but the ones that appear in the top right-hand corner (High Interest, High Power) are the people you want to manage most closely in your change process, and you may not even recognize them at first.

A woman in a graduate class I taught was working with a not-for-profit which wanted to do more outreach in the local community. The desired outcome was established, the plans made and the

Worksheet 5: Categorize Stakeholders

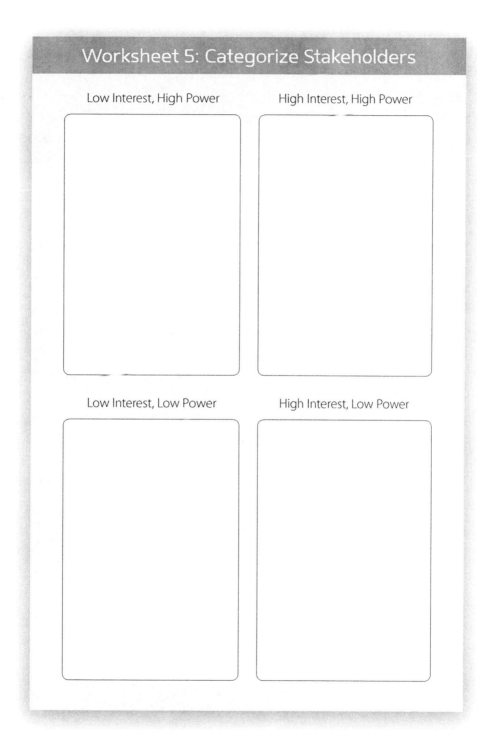

Low Interest, High Power

High Interest, High Power

Low Interest, Low Power

High Interest, Low Power

objectives set. With obstacles identified and categorized and stakeholders identified, the plan began to take shape, but there was one outspoken group of residents in the area who had been overlooked. They were not overtly wealthy or powerful, but within the neighborhood they were well known and had a great deal of clout—a different kind of high power status. As it turned out, they had a great deal of interest in the plans, too. They were able to completely derail the plans because they hadn't been consulted or asked for their support. Fortunately, subsequent meetings took place and they became allies, and ultimately became one of the main reasons the project was successful.

This story is a great example of how good plans can go awry without considering and leveraging the stakeholder interest. My students and the not-for-profit never even thought about this group, and yet they turned out to hold the key to ultimate success. It is honestly better to consider everyone, even if you end up leaving him or her out of your change process, than to miss someone or some group that holds an important stake. Clearly, it is not wise to assume you have support, or assume that you can ignore someone because he doesn't seem to care or have power. Anywhere our lives touch another person's, for right or wrong, that person may have a stake in what we're doing.

"Everyone thinks of changing the world, but no one thinks of changing himself."

—— Leo Tolstoy

CHAPTER 4

Find Your Alternatives

Now that your desired objective is clear, your obstacles highlighted and categorized, and your human factors captured, you are ready to brainstorm. Here is where you find alternatives to help you reach your desired outcome, work through your obstacles, and address any human factor issues. When I speak to large groups I'll often ask how many people thought they had a good solution to achieve a goal they had, only to find out it really wasn't a solution at all. Usually, everyone in the room raises their hands. This is again the problem with "be careful what you wish for." Someone puts a plan in place and it may or may not work, but ultimately the person didn't accomplish the true desire of his or her shift. It is something I see all too often with my business, coaching, and hypnosis clients, and my students.

The tendency is to hear the problem or the desired outcome, and then leap directly to a solution. Unfortunately, the initial solution is not always right. In some cases it is not only not the right solution;

it actually makes our lives more difficult. Of course, this isn't just for the small things in life. It can extend to the person we choose to marry, the job we covet and then find to be a poor fit, or the trip we take that ended up in food poisoning because we didn't plan appropriately and take the necessary precautions!

Defining Criteria

One more thing needs to happen before you start to brainstorm what you might do to meet your desired outcome — think about your criteria. I find that most people do this at an unconscious level, but do not capture the details on a conscious level so they can work with them.

I often use this example with my class: If you were hoping to move to a new location, what criteria might you take into account before you made a decision where to live? The students might respond with things like "being in a safe location, being close to public transportation, being somewhere warm, the cost factor, having more than one bedroom so I can have a roommate, being in the city, being close to my work or school."

When I go around and ask them to prioritize their criteria, I will obviously get different answers. One person might be adamant that the backyard has a pool, and another person might say she would never own a home with a pool! The criteria list needs to be prioritized so you are reminded of what matters to you and what factors need to be considered.

For example, when my parents sold our family home they had a prioritized checklist of what they wanted in a new location. They looked at many places and knew when they had found the one (three miles from my own home!) that fit all of their criteria. They have had few regrets about living there, because it met all of their important criteria.

As another example, let's say your shift includes exercising more and generally getting more physical activity. One of your criteria might be that since you aren't a morning person, you do not want to put this on your calendar before 6 a.m. Or maybe you aren't a gym person, so you want to find activities that do not involve going to the gym; or perhaps it is important to you that the physical activity you do is fun, so you do not feel as if it is a chore. This type of list might lead you to start thinking about having a Wii Fit in your living room for use after work—providing, of course, that one of your obstacles isn't limited space, or your stakeholders do not include children who won't let you near the television! My sister, who is a single mom and works a lot of hours, found this particular solution to work well for her—considering her obstacles, stakeholders, and criteria. She might never have thought to do this without going through the criteria process.

Again, just because we do not usually write down our criteria doesn't mean we do not have them. How many friends do you have that keep a list of what they want in a relationship? Yet that doesn't mean they do not have in mind prioritized criteria of what is important and why—even if it is often just a list of all of the things they know they do not want. We all have our criteria for every decision we make; we just do not usually catalog them in such a way that we can see them and work with them more efficiently.

Criteria often include things like time, money, physical capabilities, and interest, but depending on your desired outcome, there could be many other factors to identify.

As you work on your list of criteria, think about why different criteria are important to you. Why do you feel this item is important? What kind of priority does that item represent for you? As you put a plan in place you may have to choose something that meets only some of your criteria, so you'll want to be aware of the most critical criteria for you.

List the criteria of the desired outcome you are trying to reach—what kinds of things you want to take into account as you move toward your desired outcome. What will be the important decision-making factors that will help you decide between different alternatives?

It can be helpful to create the list, identify why the criterion matters to you, and then force a priority. Is it really a key issue for you, or are there things that you might like to have in a perfect world, but you are willing to sacrifice if you had to?

Worksheet 6: Define Criteria		
Criterion	Why is this important?	Is it a priority?

Preparing to Brainstorm

Now that you have created a list of what matters, you can begin the brainstorming process. Be sure you have the time and opportunity to focus on this before you start to think about your ideas.

Have all of the pieces to the S.H.I.F.T. Model™ to work with before you begin. Keep your desired outcome clearly in front of you before you start. Once you have taken the time to identify what the desired outcome looks like for you, post it somewhere prominent to remind yourself of your definition of success. Mine hangs next to my computer so that I look at it several times throughout the day. At the brainstorming stage, you might want to revisit what you originally wrote as your desired outcome. As you work through the additional steps, look for new information to guide you. Think about giving a bit more detail to (1) what this outcome means to you, (2) exactly what success looks like when you get there, and (3) how you will be different once you reach the goal. The important thing is to have your desired outcome written down and documented, and then find ways to keep it in front of you—literally—so you can focus on it with clarity.

To use another hypnosis technique, practice some visualization or "acting as if" before you start to brainstorm your alternatives. It can be helpful to sit in a quiet spot to do this. Close your eyes and imagine what it will be like to reach your desired outcome. Some people "see" it, others think about it, and still others just feel it. Whatever your mode may be, spend some time pretending you are at the desired outcome. This can help you make the process of reaching the goal seem more realistic and achievable. It also sets your mind and focus toward what you want, instead of on what you do not want.

Let's say you have chosen to expand your circle of friends and want to be more sociable and involved in fun activities at least once a week after work or on weekends. Try to visualize yourself at events laughing with people you enjoy, and going out dancing or to a movie (depending on what activities are meaningful for you). If you are part of a team in a company and your desired outcome is to work together more effectively and with more satisfaction to reach the department's goals, try to visualize things like communicating openly, enjoying working together, reaching your financial objectives, getting accolades from your superiors, and being happy about coming to work. This paints a clear picture that you can keep in front of you while you brainstorm.

While it was very important to capture your criteria and prioritize them as you brainstorm your options, you may find that you need to alter your criteria a bit to give you more latitude. Do this, because you might not feel as good about your outcome if it doesn't meet all of your important criteria. You are always left with the option of keeping your criteria in place and finding solutions that fit by simply disregarding anything that doesn't meet all of your criteria. This is why forcing priorities is so important. You could find a solution that meets most of your criteria but not all. The main thing is to be conscious of what you are doing. We often sacrifice something through reactive decision-making, and then we regret having done it when we realize what we have given up in the process.

Some Brainstorming Techniques

There are many types of brainstorming techniques to help you get around obstacles. If there are a few people trying to figure out what to do—your family or a study group, perhaps—you can leverage them for their thoughts. Recently I've read that some research shows people make their best decisions when they do not seek outside advice, which has to do with how we are influenced by others' thinking. So, you might want to seek input and ideas, but not ask for answers.

The objective here is to identify all of the options possible to get to your desired outcome. Having spent the time identifying your obstacles, your internal human factor, and your external stakeholders is critical. You will want to brainstorm ideas, but check them against these areas.

Carefully review what you have done so far with the S.H.I.F.T. Model™. Review your obstacles in their respective categories. Next, review the human factors: your internal feelings, concerns, and emotions, or the stakeholders you have identified, or both. Go through these lists and watch what your mind starts to do in terms of possible solutions. Sometimes ideas start to come together as you review your lists—as they did with my sister and her Wii Fit exercise ideas.

If nothing pops up when you look over your obstacles, take out a piece of paper or open a Word document and write, "What can I do?" at the top of the sheet. Then list all of the things that come to your mind. Do not qualify or judge any of your ideas at first, just get everything you think of—no matter how hokey—on paper.

Earlier I spoke about the book I wanted to write in 2009. I set this as a Desired Outcome. My obstacles were many, given that I have three kids, a full-time consulting business, a houseful of pets, and a husband, and I teach two courses per semester. It actually seemed impossible to write the book without a major impact on something.

I started the brainstorming process, though, after I had completed the first three steps of my S.H.I.F.T. Model™, and I started to get some ideas. I then captured those ideas in writing and began to feel my brain wondering, "Why do you think you can do this? This is crazy!" This was part of the human factor for me, but I forged ahead anyway and proceeded to record ideas that might be workable.

I found that one of the ideas, scheduling 45 minutes each day into my workday calendar, was a possible solution: forty-five minutes for five days a week adds up to almost four hours each week. I then considered that I could manage to block out three hours each week-end, for a total of seven hours. Now that doesn't sound like much, but given the step-by-step plan I was eventually able to create (more about that later), it ended up being plenty of time for me to write the book and complete it in the first few months of the year.

Before I began to brainstorm ideas, I thought my desired outcome was unachievable. Once I completed the process and started to list all of the things I could do, I started to see some light. The book actually became a possibility for me. Next thing I knew, it became a reality for me! Writing this book was something I had thought about doing for many, many years but until I applied the S.H.I.F.T. Model™, there was simply no way to make the progress I sought.

Beware of Naysayers

Be sure, when you are at this stage of your shifting process, that you do not share your ideas or ask for feedback on what you are trying to accomplish from people who won't be fully supportive of your endeavors. There are always people anxious to tell you why a particular approach won't work or how hopeless it is (trust me—I wrote a book about understanding people!), and they will throw cold water on your ideas before you have even had a chance to flesh them out. That isn't the case, thankfully, with everyone. You do have to guard your plans at this stage until you have had a chance to explore them and crystallize them in your own mind. I hope that when you identified your stakeholders and your internal human factors (perhaps you're the one who throws cold water on your own plans and ideas at times), you recognized this dynamic either within yourself or with certain stakeholders.

Once you have captured your potential alternatives in writing, let the list sit for a day or two. As you allow your mind to turn away from the process and focus on something else, you'll find that ideas will start to germinate on their own. Moreover, it is the same for teams. If you did use a group to generate ideas, brainstorm at one meeting, type notes and circulate them, and then schedule a next meeting to create a plan once everyone has had time to digest all the proposals.

When you come back to your list in a day or two, go through it and consider each possible solution against: (1) Your desired outcome. How do your ideas bring you closer to the outcome you desire? (2) Your obstacle list. As you look at what you can control and what you can influence, do your solutions allow you to overcome the obstacles that might be in the way? (3) Your human factor. Can you deal with this personally? Which of your stakeholders will support you in it and how? (4) Your criteria list. Which of the ideas you are considering meet your most important criteria?

You might want to create four columns next to each solution, so you can go through and consider each one against the four categories. Of course, this probably won't take a long time, because most people only have two to four possible solutions.

What Can You Do?

As you review the ideas you have brainstormed against the four categories, you should start to see which ideas seem most workable and which do not. When I went through my brainstormed list and found the idea of using 45 minutes each day and three hours on the weekend for my book project, I realized it met all of my important criteria. I immediately knew this was my best option. Does this mean it was the only way to do it, or even the best way to do it? No. But it doesn't matter—it met my needs and ultimately allowed me to meet my desired outcome.

Another example for me of how this process can work has to do with the rescued animals I love so dearly. I've always wanted to

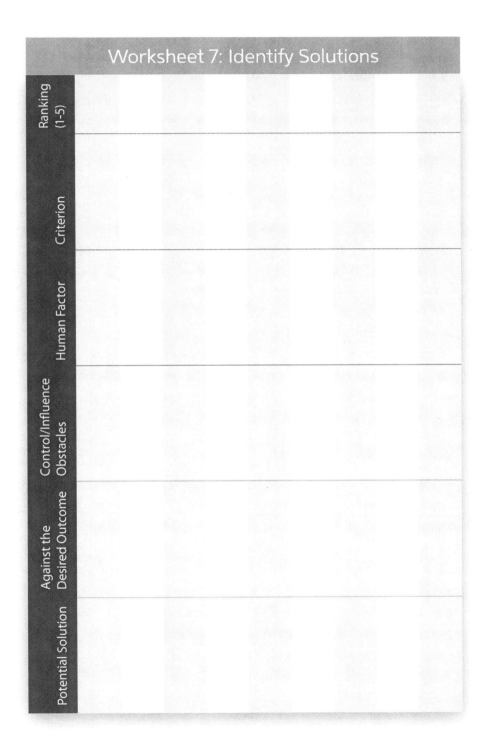

Worksheet 7: Identify Solutions

Potential Solution	Against the Desired Outcome	Control/Influence Obstacles	Human Factor	Criterion	Ranking (1-5)

volunteer in some way, but I can't work in a traditional shelter because I would be prone to bringing all of them home. I know my limitations (internal human factor) and the sadness of seeing the animals in cages week after week with nowhere to go would overwhelm me. I also know my husband won't let any more animals into our own home on a permanent basis (external stakeholder). I identified other obstacles to my desire, like not having a significant amount of extra time, and not wanting to travel too far to do the rescue work (due to the time factor and the wear and tear on me). I also wanted to avoid negative people or environments, which can be very common where there is suffering and difficulty. As I brainstormed alternatives, I found one that seemed to fit all my criteria: to find a place where the animals were in temporary shelter situations waiting to go to adoptive homes (to avoid the sadness of not being able to bring every animal home), somewhere near where I lived, and on a schedule I could accommodate. Because I had clearly identified an option that could work for me, I was able to start a search for something that met my criteria. I found the perfect match with Forever Home Rescue right in my own town. I now volunteer and clean cages on Monday mornings with a great group of very upbeat, dedicated women. All of our animals are leaving the same day to go to either adopters or volunteers, so it is actually a happy time for me. For years I had dreamed of doing something like this, but until I applied the S.H.I.F.T. Model™ I really didn't understand the different alternatives that could work for me. Now one of my favorite times of the week is Monday morning, cleaning messy cages!

Consider at this stage that you aren't seeking a single perfect answer. You are seeking the best answer that will give you the greatest possibility of reaching your desired outcome.

"Planning is bringing the future into the present
so that you can do something about it now."
— Alan Laekin

CHAPTER 5

Take Disciplined Action

If you have been successful in brainstorming a few possible ideas and you have been able to identify a solution that appears to be the best fit for your circumstances, it is time to create your plan. Of course, as you have seen throughout the book each stage has its associated difficulties, and creating the plan is no different. In business and in personal situations it is common to hear someone announce a grand idea. They can paint a picture of the idea, they can tell you all the components of the idea, and they can even engage you with their excitement and confidence, but what they can't tell you is how they are going to get from here to there, step by step, in detail. This is the most difficult part of the process in most situations, because the devil is in the details.

When I decided to write my book and I had to sit down and list all of the components in the process, it entailed everything from obtaining an ISBN, to getting a cover design, to finding a qualified editor, to every step in the marketing process and beyond. In order to use the hours I allocated effectively, I first had to capture everything that I would need to do, so I had the ability to act instead of wasting time thinking about what was next. Working with my 45-minute blocks of time, I had to know exactly what to do to be most efficient in each of those minutes.

But How Will You DO It?

In my Leadership class, when the students try to solve a problem that a business has brought to them, they will usually come up with great ideas and solutions as soon as they hear the problem the business faces. They will very excitedly share their solution to the challenge raised. That is, until I ask them how exactly they plan to implement their solution. They will often look like the proverbial deer in the headlights at that point and ask, "You mean we actually have to be the ones who take the steps necessary to put this in place?"

Whether you're dealing with a personal or a business context, taking action and, even more specifically, taking responsibility for action is crucial. In fact, it is what taking disciplined action is about, for the most part. The disciplined part comes down to actually taking responsibility and staying focused.

It is fun to create ideas and brainstorm solutions and pontificate about what we are going to do someday, but the only people who actually make the change happen are the ones who can clearly identify what next steps they will take to get them closer to their goal.

I'm continually amazed by how many people want to get somewhere but do not have a written plan as to how they are going to do it. This doesn't mean creating a plan and writing a novel about all of your ideas; it just means identifying your shift, taking into account all of the aspects you need to think about, and then determining what step-by-step actions you will take to get you from here to there.

No plan, no matter how detailed, is foolproof. Life definitely intervenes, and sometimes we have to make a mid-course correction or go down another road to get to our desired outcome. But just because there may be a need for a detour in your trip doesn't mean you do not bother with running the MapQuest® report in the first place to figure out how to get to your desired destination! And maybe you can look at the map and see exactly what to do, but most people I know really like those step-by-step directions that tell them when and where to go.

Moving to the End Goal

How does the process unfold from here? You have reviewed all of the alternatives you could come up with against your criteria, and you have decided which one you want to implement and the corresponding path you will take.

Let's look first at a simple example: You want to obtain an "A" in the graduate class you are taking. Some of your obstacles involve your full-time job, your family demands, and your lack of pleasure in the class. Your stakeholders could include your professor, your spouse, your boss, and your own internal resistance to studying for a class you do not enjoy. You have uncovered the fact that while you have the desire for the "A," you just do not devote the time necessary to study because of family factors and your own wandering interest while in the class. So you brainstorm and discover that one idea to get you to the "A" is to record (with the professor's permission) the class and read into a recorder some of the coursework you are supposed to know. You love to jog and you go out every morning, so your plan is to listen to these lectures and the book readings while you jog.

Combining a fun activity with the chance to listen to the material you need to learn can sometimes change your attitude to the material but, at minimum, it exposes you to the material when you are in a positive and open state of mind.

Your disciplined action plan might look like this:

1. Buy a recorder that you can use while running (cost assumptions included).
2. Schedule time to talk to the professor after class to ask if you can record the class; explain your desire to do well and your need to have the teachings recorded. (One note: Maybe you should not express your lack of interest in the class—as a college professor, I can tell you that this doesn't go over well!)
3. Schedule a time each evening when you can read sections of the book into your recorder.
4. Leave the recorder with your running sneakers so that you remember to take it with you when you put them on each morning.
5. Listen to the recording as you run.
6. Ask your spouse or one of your children (schedule this into your calendar) to test you on the material to see if you are actually learning.
7. Get the "A"!

While some of the steps in the process may seem self-explanatory and even basic, writing it all down in detail gives you a much greater percentage possibility of doing each of the steps. It is all too common to overlook something, and have very good intentions, but find we didn't think enough about whatever it was to include it in our plans.

Each step in the process should be broken down to its finest level of detail so that nothing is left to the vicissitudes of assumption.

Let's look at a more complicated example. Say you and your two friends get together and decide that you need to coordinate schedules and carpool to pick up kids from school. The idea finally selected is to put together a schedule of rotation.

The disciplined action might include the following:

1. Make up a list of everyone's schedules so that everyone knows which days are best for each person.
2. Set up a schedule with the dates and times for each school day.
3. Put each person's name next to each date.
4. Share the plan so that everyone can read it and approve their date/time and name, making a point of exceptions if needed.
5. Establish a backup plan in case there is one day that one of you is unavailable and needs to switch.
6. Put together a list of cell phone numbers and emergency contacts so that everyone can be reached easily.
7. Establish a plan to meet once per month or once every two months, either on the phone or in person, to discuss possible adjustments that need to be made.

Assuming that others know what we know and will do what we would do in the same situation is a dangerous flaw in many plans. Each of our styles is different; our values are different; our education, background, and knowledge levels are different, so we can't assume that because one person knows what to do in detail at a given step, everyone else does too.

To ensure effectiveness in meeting the desired outcome, the plan must be granular and specific steps must be outlined and assigned.

Break It Down!

Part of the detail is the "who" for each step. We can say "Make a list," but we also have to identify who will make the list. Who will be responsible for creating it and then circulating it? A name must be assigned to each step, along with a deadline and any resource or budget considerations.

For example, in the earlier scenario of listening to a recording while running each day, you were asked to capture the cost of buying a recorder. Anything that might derail a process, like an unanticipated expense, must be identified in advance.

This is a good discipline to develop in general, too. I've lost count of the number of times I have been in a meeting, participated in a conference call, or talked with my kids or my spouse, and we've agreed on some sort of next step, but the next step never crystallized. Agreeing on a next step is only half the process—figuring out who, what, when, how much, etc. is the other half. Without that second half of the step, time rolls on and our "meant to do that" creeps in. Because we have not taken the time to capture, record, and lay it out, we simply do not get to it. It is just too easy to move on with the other demands of life.

Many frustrating situations could have been avoided if the people looking to achieve goals had taken the time to think about the who, how, what, and when of things that needed to be done. It is so important to take the time to make sure that anyone else involved in the process of executing steps is clear on their tasks.

I'm reminded of the importance of this when I give an assignment that I believe is so clear. But regularly my students ask "How many pages? Double or single spaced? What size font do you like?" and so on. Their questions remind me how much detail we really need to offer so that we can receive the outcome we are looking for in its entirety as we want it, and when we want it.

Breaking what you need to do down into very discrete steps can also help to make the tasks more manageable. Could I write a whole book, given all of my life commitments? No, of course not! Could I come up with 45 minutes each day with a clear list of what I needed to do and complete one step each day? Yes, I could!

To help in the process of breaking it down, I have created a simple implementation plan that I use with my corporate clients and individuals to outline their disciplined action (see the next page).

This plan allows you to list each step in the process and think about who, when, how much, and so on. I find this planning process helpful even in my day-to-day to-do lists. A simple to-do item like "Plan my son's birthday party" seems like one step at first glance. But when I use the above template, I can list out all the steps in the process: Find a venue, create an invite list, order a cake, buy invitations, consider whether there will be entertainment, search online options, etc. Breaking down to-do items into discrete steps gives me a much better chance of completing what I need to. The more specific the step, the more likely I am to do it. It also helps me to find things I can delegate. I am a doer-type, so often I will just take the necessary steps on my own without thinking about who could help me. When I break my to-do's down, however, oftentimes I find there is a step I can delegate to someone else. In the example of my son's birthday, it became a family planning event as I engaged my spouse for a step or two, my older daughter to help, and our nanny to take a few steps. And because I created the plan, I could keep the fun steps for myself and still get everything done!

Have you ever read a book about getting clutter out of your life? This seems to be a chronic problem, and there is an abundance of books on the subject. Pick up any one of them and the author will tell you not to think about cleaning the whole house at once, but rather about starting in one corner at a time. There are two reasons for this: first, because we feel a sense of accomplishment if we take on something and complete it, and second, because it reduces the job so it seems more doable. Rather than getting all of the drawers pulled out

Worksheet 8: Breaking Down the Details

Discrete step in the process	Who will do this?	By when?	Is there a cost? If so, how much?	What else needs to be considered at this step?

in every room and then being unable to complete the process, taking one small corner and finishing it in the allocated time actually gets something done. Of course, in my house with three kids, a husband, a houseful of pets, and a busy life, it seems like all the corners have clutter, but that's beside the point. Fortunately, having a neat home hasn't yet made it onto my list of desired outcomes!

So to recap, the process of breaking down the plan into specific, discrete steps is where you finally take your disciplined action. Your plan should outline your target dates and who will help you and what you need to do. Keep this plan visible, even if it means carrying it in your wallet or purse. You may want to transfer each of the steps to an Outlook® or Google™ calendar, or some other task list you rely on. Each day that you need to complete something, you should have the step clearly defined and incorporated into your calendar so that it isn't an "if," but rather a "when." Do not leave anything to chance at this stage of the process. You have worked hard on each step of shifting to this point, and this is where you need to commit to breaking down your steps and finding ways to work through each part of your daily, weekly, or monthly plan. You know what you need to do, so set deadlines and assign steps in the process to others wherever you can.

Having a method to capture what you need to do, and to keep yourself on track, is imperative to your success with this process. Once you have your plan, review it and be sure you have a detailed timeline associated with what you need to do. Do that right now, and before you do anything else, take those dates and write them in your calendar. That binds you to a written commitment and confirms the time and date of what you will do and how you will do it.

Determine other methods that will help you keep on track. For many people, writing on 3 × 5 cards works well (this is my personal favorite). I put the steps I need to take on cards and keep them taped to my computer and on my bathroom mirror. They remind me of what I am striving toward and what I need to do at each step.

Having a "buddy" works well for some people. The idea is to let that person know what you are striving toward — your definition of success — and then to commit to that person what you will do and when you will do it. There really is some magic to making a commitment to someone else, because we tend to take it more seriously than we do a commitment to ourselves. Your buddy can be a roommate, spouse, or friend — or it could be someone online you keep in contact with through Facebook® or LinkedIn®.

Some people find using a tickler system very helpful. My husband is a big fan of the "Getting Things Done®" (GTD) approach by David Allen, and everything he commits to goes into his GTD® system. He uses that software and his Outlook calendar to remind him of dates and commitments.

Color-coded folders are yet another approach. I once worked with an organizer who showed me that buying a label maker was the best investment I could make! I have color-coded folders for different projects (clients, books, marketing, financial information), and I can create a separate folder for each specific project. For example, this book has its own folder, in which I keep a list of when, and what, I need to do, so I can refer back to it at any point.

There are many, many systems and approaches. Becoming very good at time management can be useful, and in my experience those who are good at managing their time always have some sort of system they use to keep them on track.

So, make your commitment. Create your plan. Find the way to keep yourself on track and make your shift happen!

Congratulations! If you have come this far in the book, you have created your plan for shifting. In my work with people in their personal lives and in businesses, there are many other factors that I see contributing to one's overall level of success and contentedness. In the second part of this book, I want to share some ideas to consider for an overall increase in effectiveness.

Tips and Tools for Greater Effectiveness in Life

As I've worked with many different types of people at all different stages of their lives, and with my hypnosis and coaching clients trying to improve some facet of their lives, I've identified a few key areas that every person can benefit from, no matter what their status in life or where they are trying to get to.

Part II holds many keys from programs, coaching work, training sessions, and one-to-one work that I've done over the years. I've taken the best ideas and put them in this book so that you can read one, practice with it, and improve in that particular area.

As you try out some of the ideas here, do not lose sight of your overall desire to shift. These ideas and improvements can aid you in the process, but you will still want to follow the S.H.I.F.T. Model™ for long-lasting and significant success.

*"All changes, even the most longed for, have their melancholy;
for what we leave behind us is a part of ourselves; we must
die to one life before we can enter another."*

— Anatole France

CHAPTER 6

Create a Meaningful Shift

The law of attraction is a theory that suggests we draw things into our lives according to what we focus our energies on. It posits that we create our own circumstances by the choices we make in life, and those choices are fueled by our thoughts. What this boils down to is: Our thoughts are the most powerful tools we have. And honestly, this is a fundamental posit for most goal setting and just about every effort to understand what drives successful change. When you focus on something you want, you are likely to get it.

The law of attraction, like just about any other form of goal setting, actually encourages you to know who you are and what you are attracting into your life. You need to examine very closely what you're feeling and why. You also need to look into changing your feelings, if they are negative, by finding the root cause of the problem and dealing with it head-on.

Here are some tips you can take from this. First, most people focus on the present and talk about their current reality. They reinforce problems when they concentrate on them in a negative way. The problem with focusing on the present——concentrating on, for instance, being overweight——is that you enforce unhappiness with this situation. The more you think about negative elements of your life without thinking about how you can change them, the more you focus on it and talk about it, the more you reinforce the negativity in your life.

Concentrate on stopping negative feelings about problems. Instead, recognize that you are willing to work hard to make your life better, to make a shift in the first place, and use this to motivate your shift process.

I learned a wonderful technique and I use it frequently in my hypnosis work——it is the STOP! Technique. This technique requires you to be aware of the negative thoughts you allow into your mind. When you do recognize the same old self-defeating tape playing repeatedly, put up the imaginary STOP! sign. You literally see a big red sign in your mind, and you can say to yourself (or out loud if conditions allow it) "STOP!" You are telling your own mind to cease and desist. It can be useful to have a replacement thought or little ditty that you repeat over and over. I am a music lover, so I have refrains from upbeat songs that I love. When I need to use the STOP! approach, I tell myself to stop and then start singing some song that I enjoy. It sounds silly, but it works!

You do not want to put on rose-colored glasses and tell yourself everything is wonderful when it isn't, but you do want to gain your own energy back to deal with whatever comes your way. The negative refrains zap our energy and leaving us feeling like "Why bother?" at times.

As you work to identify your desired outcome, try to recognize what your thoughts, feelings, and actions are driving you to.

Visualizing your future life can help you figure out what desired outcomes you really want. Catching yourself defeating yourself along the way can help to get you back on track.

Knowing yourself, your thoughts and feelings, is central to taking control of your life. Gratitude is an example of a magnetic force in the universe. Nothing new can come into your life unless you open yourself up to being grateful for what you already have. This perspective applies to all elements of your life; financial status, family, friends, and other aspects of life. There is nothing more powerful than taking a few minutes—when you are feeling low—to list what you do have in your life. If you do not feel like you have much, start with the breath you take every day. Life itself is a gift, even though we choose not to open it most days!

"Every day, in every way, I am getting better and better."
— Emile Coue

CHAPTER 7

Look in the Mirror — and Smile!

To create a meaningful shift, knowing yourself, and what you want, is perhaps the first thing. The second, perhaps, is recognizing your strengths and weaknesses and how they tend to impact what you do, how they have brought you to where you are today.

It is interesting that a lot of us think we can shame ourselves into being different. We think criticism and harsh judgments will improve the aspects of ourselves with which we are unhappy. As a strategy, though, this rarely works. Beating up on anyone is never an effective motivator! Beating up on yourself is no less effective.

Disparagement is not motivating; it makes most people defensive and resistant. To create balance in your life and to secure the things you want, it is important to stop focusing on your flaws and shortcomings. Begin to shift your efforts and start recognizing your strengths, talents, and other positive qualities even as you prepare to shift toward your goals.

You need a balanced view of yourself, but change can occur most readily and most effectively when you have a personal foundation of self-acceptance and support——a committed and nurturing relationship with yourself.

Unfortunately, society and, more specifically, the stakeholders in our lives, do not support this notion. We have all overheard conversations about a conceited person——how someone else has a swelled head. We have already identified naysayers as people to avoid as you pursue your shift, but I emphasize here that they should be avoided altogether. When we receive a compliment, in many instances, we feel it is better to underplay the achievement: We say "it is nothing" or we try to deflect the praise. There is definitely a fine line between confidence and ego, but it must be walked. I have found that the most successful people combine a healthy sense of confidence with the humility that comes from a willingness to learn about oneself.

To achieve goals that are meaningful to you, however, it is important to understand and appreciate your own talents and strengths, because this will let you become more confident and centered in your life and thus better able to see what will be, for you, a beneficial and valuable change.

On the flip side, though, you have to understand your own weaknesses, too. It is not effective to just pretend they aren't there——that's ego! More than this, you have to go to work on them; face them head on. The purpose of evaluating your weaknesses is not to make you feel miserable or frustrated. In the same way, recognizing your strengths isn't designed to make you conceited.

Try, as best you are able, not to shy away from your weaknesses. Instead, you should recognize them for what they are: areas of yourself that need improvement. Look at your weaknesses objectively; admit to them. Try to understand where they originated and, if they are holding you back, make a conscious effort to turn them around.

"I try to take one day at a time, but sometimes several days attack me at once."
—Jennifer Yane

CHAPTER 8

Managing Your Stress

Many people find that their energy is zapped by evening because of the stress that grinds them down throughout the day. That might even be your primary area of focus, if your desired outcome includes "Living with less stress and feeling more relaxed and confident each day." Unfortunately, for most people stress is a fact of life, something that just circulates and colors everything else but never really leaves you alone.

Stress comes in many forms. There is so-called "good stress" that motivates us and drives us to reach new heights, and then there is "bad stress" that consumes us and makes us less effective in our day-to-day activities. I believe that any unmanaged and unwanted stress is bad stress, so I am going to review some options for diminishing it. Emotional stress factors are just as painful as physical stress factors, and must be considered and treated gently.

The right approach to managing stress has much to do with our behavioral style. A person who is a high-energy, physically active, and fast-moving type of person will need to dissipate their energy by physical activities — by taking a run, climbing a mountain, cardio-boxing, and the like. Someone who is more laid-back, quiet, and unemotional in style will need quiet time or alone time to recharge his or her batteries. When the two styles are married to one another and both people are stressed, this can create new stress in and of itself. If, for example, I relieve stress by mountain biking with my spouse, but my spouse just wants to relieve stress by quietly reading the newspaper in the den, our disagreement about what we need to do in our shared time may add to the stress!

Be aware of what you need to do to relieve stress, and work to feed that part of yourself on a regular basis. If I first identify how I can best recharge my batteries, then I can find ways to work those activities into my life. It comes back to having a plan. If I realize I am starting to be too pulled and too triggered, I may want to prioritize activities that are de-stressing to me. What I do not want to do is ignore the warning signs until I find myself sick or unable to cope because I didn't act on those warnings.

Just Breathe!

Learning to breathe is so important for stress reduction. One of my clients went to a coaching program for a week and came back very excited. He told me that after almost 50 years, he finally learned how to breathe! Unbelievably, learning how to breathe effectively made a significant difference in his feelings about his work, his family, and his life.

In hypnosis we focus a lot on breathing the right way. Here is a simple way to help you learn effectively how to take deep, cleansing breaths. Close your eyes for a minute and imagine a blue balloon in your stomach. Imagine that the balloon is deflated and you will inflate it with your breath. Breathe in deeply through your nose and focus on filling that balloon to its most round state. Breathe in very deeply but not so deeply that you get light-headed. This should be comfortable, not something that adds to your stress! As you gently breathe in, imagine the balloon filling up with air. Once it is filled, release the air through your mouth. Remember that rather than breathing into your diaphragm, as most of us have learned to do, you are breathing in and out from your stomach. Allow the breath to fill you, and then release it. Do this at least 3-4 times until you can feel your entire body relaxing. Whenever you get into a strained situation, use this breathing technique. It immediately draws your attention away from what is stressing you and toward your breath. We can't focus our minds on two things at once, so if you are focused on your breathing, you can't focus on how worried you are about your boss having called you into his office. The act of focusing on breathing turns your attention to your breath, instead of the concern or thought that is distracting. In order to have a more confident and decisive approach, clear your mind of the distractions that impede focus.

Take your time to breathe this way before facing any potentially stressful or worrisome situation. At first, the act of breathing will require your attention. Once you are breathing comfortably, you can start to turn your attention to whatever it is you need to deal with at that time. Your breathing allows you the clarity and focus you need to think about the problem or issue in a more rational and logical manner.

Another important way to alleviate stress is to take breaks throughout the day. It is hard to sit for hours on end, or stand at a machine or in a showroom for hours, without some kind of a break. Even if you just walk into a bathroom, close the stall door, and sit down on a closed toilet to do your breathing exercise, it creates a mental and physical break in your day. Because of my career I tend to sit a lot at a computer, as I am doing now, just typing. I also spend hours talking on the phone. In fact, my kids say I get paid to "talk and type!" Because of these activities, my arms often hurt and my back gets very stiff. During my breaks, I stand up and reach my arms up as far as I can. I roll my head from side to side, just to move my muscles in a new direction. Allowing your body and your mind some sort of break in the action can bring you back to your task with a renewed focus. When I really feel the stress creeping in, I may drop what I am doing and if I am at home, grab one of the dogs for a quick run around the block. At work, I'll go downstairs to the coffee shop. I might not even buy anything, but just giving myself the mental and physical break helps.

Do your best to dispense with worry, especially as you move toward your desired goals. When I was 19 years old I read a story by Zig Ziglar, the famous motivational speaker. He quoted the writer David Mamet who said, "Worry is interest paid in advance on a debt that never comes due."

Zig advised his readers to make lists of things that worry them so they were out of mind and onto paper for planning purposes, or thrown out entirely. I resolved to become less of a worrier and more of a planner. Over time I have faced things that I wouldn't have thought I could possibly deal with, but by making a plan instead of worrying I have always been able to find ways to shift to a new situation. Some people seem to think that worry is like a cloak that will protect them, as if worrying about it enough will stop it from happening. But how much energy is spent during the worrying process? Especially if whatever you're worrying about never actually happens! If the feared trouble does happen, you need all of your energy and faculties to deal with it most effectively, do you not? So try to catch yourself whenever you find yourself giving energy over to worry states. Ask yourself what you are worrying about and whether it is something you could use the S.H.I.F.T. Model™ to deal with. Worrying, if you can turn it into a trigger that helps you plan, can be productive.

A common dynamic with some professional people I work with occurs when there are changes looming in their work environment and they are feeling the fear of what might happen to them. Fear of the unknown overwhelms them, and they find themselves fixating on the worst possibility of what could go wrong. When this dynamic takes shape, the process of worrying hampers their ability to be a top performer, because the worry begins to permeate their day-to-day abilities. Someone who may have been competent and confident is now slinking by their manager's door or fearfully watching the faces of senior managers in a meeting. His or her fear takes on a life of its own, and the person could be labeled as someone who isn't confident enough for the next phase of the business, or even put on a list to be let go! Ultimately the worry has turned into a self-fulfilling prophecy.

Likewise, I've worked with single people who are in a relationship and spend a lot of time worrying about whether their significant other is really interested in them or is going to stick around. The worry and the ensuing behavior it often brings about can sometimes drive the other person away.

I've come to understand that there aren't a lot of good reasons to worry, and that it takes a toll on our emotional and physical strength when we let it consume us. Finding ways to focus your attention on more positive steps to take will ultimately benefit you much more than worrying will, no matter what you are facing.

To the degree that you can keep away from people who are gloom and doom, or away from reading undesirable things or watching TV programs with dire predictions, you will find you may be less worried in general. I'm not suggesting denial is a good state to be in, but if you are a person prone to worry, exposing yourself to those things that create more pointless fear and concern may be counterproductive. For example, one year my son's Boy Scout group went on a Ghost Walk. It sounded like fun to me, so I agreed to take the place of one of the troop leader moms and go with the boys. I'm not afraid of ghosts myself, so I thought it was a nice time and I enjoyed learning about the history of many "true" ghost stories in this particular area. However, one boy on the walk had a latent fear of ghosts and the "undead" that both his family and I were unaware of. He didn't sleep for several months after the ghost tour. This was a good lesson for me. In this boy's case no one knew the fear was there, but if you know something upsets you, by all means, stay away from it unless your desired outcome is to overcome that particular fear!

Create a Positive Trigger

One last idea for stress reduction is to learn self-hypnosis techniques, like developing a positive trigger for when you face something that concerns you. Sitting in a quiet spot and taking three deep breaths can accomplish this. Close your eyes on the third breath and just sit there, being aware of your breathing and how it calms you. As you sit, continue to focus on your breath and to breathe in and out as your body adjusts and becomes more relaxed. Once you feel you are truly relaxed, put the first three fingers of your right or left hand (thumb, pointer finger, and middle finger) together as your "trigger," or reminder. Allow these three fingers to touch one another at the same time at the tips. Hold this position as you continue to breathe and feel relaxed. Quietly say to yourself, "I am calm. I am relaxed. I am in control. My three fingers remind me that I am calm, I am relaxed, I am in control. Because I have identified this as a trigger, every time I put my three fingers together, I will remember to be calm, relaxed, and in control." As you say this to yourself, continue to breathe, hold your fingers together, and see yourself as calm and confident.

Practice this a few times each day until you can put your three fingers together with your eyes open and allow the mental "trigger" to calm your body. For years and years I used this technique before I made a speech. I was never afraid — I actually enjoy public speaking — but I always felt a degree of nervousness right before I would walk out on the stage. I would look out at the audience and start to worry about getting cold feet. Putting my three fingers together at my side allowed me to calm down and feel in control as I began speaking. Once I was into my speech, I would continue to become more and more relaxed. Over the years, I have developed into what I hope is an excellent public speaker, and as I've stated before it is one of the things I most enjoy doing. Even now, from time to time when an event is really big and very important, I still find myself unconsciously putting my fingers together before I walk up on the stage.

"You have power over your mind—not outside events. Realize this, and you will find strength."
— Marcus Aurelius

CHAPTER 9

Finding Your Breakthrough

Another important skill in effective goal setting and creating an effective shift is to identify and break through any destructive patterns that emerge in life. These can come from anywhere. They might emerge in relationships—in general or in a specific relationship, such as your relationship with your spouse or with a parent. You might also find that destructive patterns emerge in your career or in other areas of your personal life.

In Part I, I discussed how destructive patterns can offset your ability to achieve goals. For instance, if you have a tendency to eat sweet foods at night—snack on cookies and milk at bedtime, for instance—you might well be dealing with a destructive pattern: a craving for carbs or sugary foods, for instance, that, unless you address it directly, is going to throw you off your goals every time.

However, what do you do when you are dealing with destructive patterns in a particular area of your life? There can be little doubt that such patterns are damaging, at the very least because they tend to undermine your self-confidence, your belief that you might actually be able to go ahead and make positive shifts.

Whether you are dealing with an issue that is harming your health, anxiety is undermining your relationships, or some other kind of obstacle is repeatedly showing up in your life, you need some direct action to break the destructive patterns as you strive to create your shift.

Review why you want to change. Throughout this book, I've stressed the importance of motivation and of identifying the right kind of goals for you. The first step in breaking destructive patterns is emphasizing to yourself why you are making the change. How much do you really value moving to a new place? In the S.H.I.F.T. Model™, I identify commitment and motivation as two overriding drivers. You must have them in place if you really want to change. Force yourself to identify what the change means to you and how committed you really are to it.

Change your perceptions. Perceptions are very important when dealing with obstacles and destructive patterns. If your quest to get somewhere new is often interrupted or if setting goals is being undermined by destructive patterns, you need a shift. Do not dwell on the extent to which the obstacles undermine your shifts. Instead, start looking at obstacles as something to work around, to incorporate into your goal setting. Start looking at destructive patterns in the same way, as things you have to find a way to work around or simply eradicate. This is where the idea of reframing can be helpful. If you find yourself reacting to something negatively, ask yourself if there is a reframe. Can you take the same situation, or set of "facts," and view them differently to change your perception? Could the nosy neighbor be a caring, lonely individual? Could the aggressive boss be a scared person who uses anger as a shield? These things may or may not be true, but as my wonderful friend Janet Britcher, president of Transformation Management, says, "If you are going to make something up, it may as well be something good!"

Stop the cycle of generational dysfunction. As you find a way to work around or even with obstacles, address dysfunctional patterns head-on by trying to identify the underlying issues, the things driving you to repeat patterns. An example is when you notice something negative about your family dynamics—but you repeat it anyway. One of my coaching clients said to me, "I hated how my mom yelled at us constantly and now I do the same thing." Great! She identified this—now she can take steps, in the moment of yelling, to make a different choice. The STOP! Technique works here, too.

Form positive habits. Perhaps the best way to break destructive patterns is simply to form new, positive patterns to replace the negative ones. Think about shifting the way you approach issues affected by destructive patterns, such as relationships, diets, and so forth. If on the way to work you always go by the coffee shop that has the cakes you love and you just have to stop in... take a different path to work. If you find yourself ready to respond negatively to your spouse because you "just know" what they are going to say... stop and listen instead. My corporate client Ross Ozer pointed out to me that the letters in the word "listen" can be moved around to make the word "silent." Stop getting ready to respond, and just focus on the other person by being silent sometimes.

Forgive yourself. Avoid dwelling on your weaknesses or failings by forgiving yourself and admitting that obstacles and destructive patterns affect everyone. Everyone has weaknesses. Most of us are doing the best we can at any given time. We'd all like to do things differently, but we often make bad choices. You can't fix the past, so it is most useful to just forgive yourself and focus on achieving a more positive, confident future.

Stay focused. Remain focused on moving beyond your past difficulties and creating new, healthier patterns. Continue to focus on the importance of your shift, of the S.H.I.F.T. Model™. Do not become discouraged if your progress seems slow. Remember that even Albert Einstein said, "It is not that I'm so smart, it is just that I stay with problems longer." If it is good enough for Einstein, it should be good enough for you!

"Life is not easy for any of us. But what of that? We must have perseverance and above all confidence in ourselves. We must believe that we are gifted for something and that this thing must be attained."

— Marie Curie

CHAPTER 10

Building Confidence to Promote Shifts

Now let's consider confidence, self-confidence in particular, and the role that it plays in helping you make a positive shift in your life. Research shows that people learn, change, and improve the most in those areas of the brain that already have the strongest synaptic connections. You learn new things and achieve more by working from your strengths. Focusing on your strengths to develop your confidence and personal endurance will increase your performance. The better you are able to stick with the task in hand, the more likely you are to succeed at what you set out to achieve.

You have learned some of the benefits of recognizing your strengths in life and applying your strengths to benefit your efforts at change. You likely have had many great ideas in your life. You may have realized how good an idea was, as well. You might even have thought about implementing it. Still, if you're reading this book, the chances are you have not yet managed to follow through on things that are really meaningful to you.

It may be that your ideas were very sound, but you lacked the inner sense of "I can do this!" to complete them. Self-confidence is sorely lacking, in my experience, for most of the population.

Being confident in yourself often depends on the things we have discussed already, things like being self-aware, knowing who you are, being in touch with what you want, understanding your strengths and weaknesses, and knowing that how you use your given talents is the best indicator of how successful you can be.

How do we work to build our self-confidence? Some suggestions:

1. Write down three to five things you did well each day before you go to bed. Read these aloud to yourself so they are the last thing you think about before you go to sleep.

2. List ten smaller things you can do in a day to build your confidence, then work to make these things daily habits.

3. Learn something new related to your desired outcome or what is important to you. Learning new things will increase your overall confidence level.

4. Remember that confidence comes from taking risks. Do not be afraid to take risks, even when you do not yet feel confident in yourself. Confidence will come slowly.

5. Work to appreciate who you are and what you already have. Keep that gratitude list where you can look at it often.

6. Start repeating positive affirmations every day, when you wake up and before you go to sleep.

7. Identify those elements for your personal "zone"—what it feels like when you do something well.

8. When you do something you feel good about, record it right then. Keep a running list over time that you can refer to when you feel down.

"To effectively communicate, we must realize that we are all different in the way we perceive the world and use this understanding as a guide to our communication with others."
— *Tony Robbins*

CHAPTER 11

Understanding Behavioral Styles

A s I travel and speak on hundreds of radio and television shows and in-person interviews, I hear stories over and over again about the difficult people everyone has to deal with in his or her life. The truth is that there will always be people who do things that we do not necessarily consider positive. But it is the impact we allow people to have on us, or the inability we may have to deal with those people, that ultimately creates the difficulty for us. If we learn about our own style, and we can identify the style of others, it sometimes gives us more choices in relationships.

People who have read my previous book will know how important behavioral style is, but I reiterate it here because our communication style has a tremendous impact on how we are perceived and received by others. As a certified behavioral analyst, I use the DISC tool in my work. DISC identifies four facets to communication: how we deal with problems and challenges, how we interact with people, how we handle steady pace and work environment, and how we deal with rules and procedures specifically set by others.

The DISC (D for Dominance, the Problems scale; I for Influencing, the People scale; S for Steadiness, the Pace scale; and C for Compliance, the Procedures and Rules scale) formula has been around for well over 30 years. DISC allows us to categorize types of behavioral styles. If I am high on the Problems scale (meaning that I like to take on problems and challenges), I will come across much more aggressively than someone who is lower on this scale and likes to be more thoughtful and methodical about going after a problem. On the People scale, we have those who derive their energy from being around people and like to verbalize and be engaged, while others would prefer to talk less and whose energy is drained by too many human interactions. The Pace scale has people who are very high-energy and who like to move from thing to thing and seek out change, while others prefer structure, less emotion, and a more methodical, step-by-step approach. On the Rules scale, the difference is between those who like to follow the rules (such as auditors, compliance experts, or airplane mechanics) and those who seek new, creative ways to do things and may go around the rules in the process.

We all have preferences on each of the four scales to one degree or another. What is important to understand is that each of us tends to feel that our way and our style of doing things is the "best" way and maybe even the only way. The sometimes-uncomfortable truth is that we tend to like people who are like us—it is much easier for me to communicate with you, for example, if we share similarities and "click" easily because you "get" me.

When another person has a very dissimilar style to our own, we can sometimes have difficulty communicating. Many relationships struggle because the two people involved have trouble hearing each other. They both interpret the other person's communication through their own behavioral filter, and assume they know what the other is saying. Often they are surprised to learn that they've been talking past each other. It is not always just what we say, it is often how we say it that someone is keying in on. In fact, there is research that suggests the words we use are less than 10% of what someone really hears when they listen to us. The other 90%+ is body language, tone of voice, gestures, style, and approach.

Whether presenting to another person, negotiating, trying to win a sale, or simply having a respectful conversation, we have to pay attention to the other person's style. If I am a fast talker, I may need to slow down if I want to connect with a slower speaker. If I am very rules-oriented and believe that rules should be followed at all costs, I will have difficulty connecting with someone who thinks "rules are made to be broken."

There is so much information that you can gain to help you learn more about your own preferences and how to modify your own communication style and approach in order to better enable communication with others. This book isn't intended to be a guide for communication in relationships. If you want to delve into that more deeply, I'll refer you to my previous work, "Understanding Other People: The Five Secrets to Human Behavior" (www.understandingotherpeople.com). Suffice it to say that the most successful people are typically those who know and understand their own communication style, and how they are perceived, and are able to read the style of others. It is the basis for connection in our relationships and can have a large impact on how easily we can work, play, and interact with others!

More than this, though, by learning to understand yourself and those around you, how they behave and what their personality amounts to, you will be empowered with understanding. You will be able to appreciate why people react differently in different situations. Eventually, you will be better able to accept and understand people's behaviors that differ from your own. These insights will make you much more centered and better able to deal with people. You will also come to understand the all-too-important reality that you cannot be responsible for other people's behavior. The only behavior you can control is your own.

WHAT ARE YOUR GOALS?

Now that you have read all of the information in Part II, it can be helpful to go back through each section and identify where you might be able to improve in a certain area. Does stress often weigh you down? Would you like to be a more clear and confident communicator? Do you want to worry less and be more productive? These things can become desired outcomes in and of themselves, and perhaps some of what you have learned here in Part II presents you with an opportunity to go back to the S.H.I.F.T. Model™ and move in a new direction on any of these things. At a minimum, all of these areas represent an opportunity to become better in both personal and professional situations.

"Begin doing what you want to do now. We are not living in eternity. We have only this moment, sparkling like a star in our hand — and melting like a snowflake."
— Marie Beyon Rey

CHAPTER 12

Getting From There to Here

Now that you have completed all of the steps in the process, review what you have done in each section and capture it in one place.

Specify your desired outcome. Paint a clear and understandable picture of what you most desire and what success will look like when you get there. Remember to consider why this outcome is important for you to reach at this particular point in time. Evolve the desired outcome as much as you can, while keeping it realistic and measurable in some way so that you'll know that you have achieved it when you get there. Think about all of the components of what matters to you. Start by using the SMART process if this is helpful, but be sure to take into account the many aspects of where you want to go that matter to you.

Highlight your obstacles and categorize them. What prevents you from doing what you most desire today, this minute? What stands in your way? Brainstorm the things that have held you back in the past and the things you know might stand in your way as you make your shift toward your desired outcome. First list them and then categorize them: those you can control, those you can't control but can influence, and those you can't control.

Identify your internal and external human factors. First think about the internal aspect — what worries, fears, or concerns do you have? What holds you back? Conversely, what strengths do you have that will benefit you? What gives you your positive attributes? Next look at the external stakeholders — who will care about the decisions you make, and what stake do they have in them? Remember to place the stakeholders on the scale of low to high interest and low to high power.

Find your alternatives. Keep in mind all of what you have uncovered and captured in the first three steps of the process as you decide which options work for you. What are the possible ways for you to reach the desired outcome? What criteria do you have? How do you prioritize your criteria? What is most important to you? As you consider your criteria and review your list of possible alternatives, which one emerges as the best probability for making your shift?

Take disciplined action. Break it down into very discrete steps that show you clearly where you need to go, and what steps to take to get there. What is your plan? What are the specific things you need to do that will help you get there from here in a step-by-step fashion? Who needs to take some of the steps? By when? What will you do when you encounter an obstacle along the way? Be as clear and detailed as possible, and then transfer the steps into some sort of process that works for you.

About the Author

Beverly D. Flaxington is an accomplished business consultant, corporate coach, trainer, facilitator, behavioral expert, hypnotherapist, college professor, and business development expert.

Bev co-founded The Collaborative, a sales and marketing consultancy, and is currently principal of the firm. Beverly is the creator of "The Sales Effectiveness Model" used by many client firms to help diagnose areas of weakness and implement more effective selling practices. She trademarked the S.H.I.F.T. Model™ for goal setting, and The Five Secrets to Successful Selling™ program.

Beverly is a Certified Professional Behavioral Analyst (CPBA) and Certified Professional Values Analyst (CPVA). She uses the DISC and PIAV tools frequently in her work with individuals and organizations. Beverly's book, *Understanding Other People: The Five Secrets to Human Behavior*, won a gold award from Readers Favorite for best new book on relationships. She authored *The 7 Steps to Effective Business Building for Financial Advisors*. She is also the co-author of *Wealthbuilding: A Consumer's Guide to Making Profitable—and Comfortable—Investment Decisions*, published by Dearborn Financial Publishing.

Bev is a frequent contributor in the media and has been featured on:

Lifetime Television's Balancing Act, with Jordan Rich on WBZ Radio, on Doc Michelle of LA Talk Radio with Dr. Jackie Black of BlogTalk Radio, and on WVOL 1470 AM, Nashville, TN: "Differences" with Deniece Barnes; WEUS 810 AM, Orlando, FL: "The Shannon Burke Show"; WFSX 92.5 FM Fox News Radio, Ft. Meyers-Naples, FL: with Doug Kellett; KKZZ 1400 AM, Ventura, CA: with Billy Frank aka Billy The Brain; WBT 1110 AM/99.3 FM, Charlotte, NC: "Morning News Weekend" with Don Russell; CRN (Cable Radio Network): "The Talk Back Show with Chuck Wilder"; KAHI 950 AM, Auburn/Sacramento, CA: KAHI Noon News with Dave Rosenthal; KBIQ Q102.7 FM, Colorado Springs, CO: with Megan Goodyear; WCUB 980 AM/WLTU 92.1 FM, Multiple Cities, WI: "The Breakfast Club" with Dean & Bryan; KAHI 950 AM, Auburn/Sacramento, CA: "PoppOff" with Mary Jane Popp; WINA 1070 AM, Charlottesville, VA: "The Schilling Show" with Rob Schilling; KPCW 91.9 FM, Park City, UT: with Larry Warren; CRN (Cable Radio Network): The Gary Baumgarten Report; WONC 89.1 FM, Naperville, IL: "Newsmakers"; CVBT (Central Valley Business Times): with Doug Caldwell; WCHE 1520 AM, West Chester, PA: "The WCHE Wake Up Call" with Matt Lombardo; KRLD, Dallas, TX: with Bonnie Petrie and Dave Rancken.

Articles about her and her views have appeared in:

The Boston Globe, Reader's Digest, Selling Power Magazine, and SheKnows.com with Michele Borboa; Opposing Views.com with Mike McNulty; FoxNews.com; ABCNews.com

Ready for more?

Visit Bev at **www.understandingotherpeople.com** and at **www.the-collaborative.com** to learn more about workshops, products, and facilitation services or to hire Bev to speak at your company.

To learn more about communicating effectively in both work and personal settings, get a copy of Bev's book, *Understanding Other People: The Five Secrets to Human Behavior.*

CPSIA information can be obtained at www.ICGtesting.com
Printed in the USA
BVOW012157180112

280898BV00003B/6/P